MOUNT BACHELOR

MOUNT BACHELOR

· A HISTORY ·

GLENN VOELZ

THE
History
PRESS

Published by The History Press
Charleston, SC
www.historypress.com

Front cover, top: Skier on Bachelor Butte, circa 1960. *Photograph by Ray Atkeson. Copyright Ray Atkeson Image Archive. Front cover, bottom*: View of Mount Bachelor from above Todd Lake. *Photograph by Tom Iraci.*

First published 2023

Manufactured in the United States

ISBN 9781467151825

Library of Congress Control Number: 2022950082

CONTENTS

LAND ACKNOWLEDGEMENT

The forty-fourth parallel of north latitude bisects the highest point of the Egan Cone on Mount Bachelor's north slope. That line divides two of Oregon's most extensive territorial concessions of the nineteenth century.

From the top of Egan Cone, look to the north, and you see the lands ceded to the United States government by the Warm Springs and Wasco Tribes in 1855. That treaty forced the tribes to relinquish over ten million acres of land between the Columbia River and the northern slope of Bachelor Butte, extending east into the Blue Mountains. The treaty consigned the tribes to occupy around one-twentieth of their original lands on what is now the Warm Springs Reservation.

From the same point atop Egan Cone, look to the south, and you see the lands ceded by the Klamath and Modoc Tribes and the Yahooskin-Paiute people in 1864. This concession included most of Mount Bachelor and virtually everything that could be seen to the south from its summit. The tribes lost twenty-three million acres of their homeland stretching across south-central Oregon in exchange for roughly one million acres of reservation land in the Upper Klamath Basin.

Between 1853 and 1864, most of Oregon's tribes were forcibly relocated to reservations through unequal treaties, clearing the way for Euro-American settlement. Those agreements rarely included rights for Native tribes to hunt and fish in their traditional homelands and instead relegated them to life on reservations. Subsequent waves of Euro-American settlers introduced disease and land-use regimes that decimated Indigenous populations and dramatically altered their ways of life.

This land acknowledgement recognizes Mount Bachelor's place within the ancestral homelands of Oregon's Indigenous peoples. Their history on the mountain began long before Euro-American settlers first climbed its slopes and called it by their names.

A NOTE ON TERMINOLOGY

Central Oregonians continue to debate Mount Bachelor's proper name. This history does not attempt to settle that argument. Nevertheless, an explanation of the naming convention used in this book is necessary to avoid confusion.

It is unclear exactly when the name Bachelor Butte came into everyday use. Early Bend pioneer John C. Todd remembered locals referring to it as Brother Jonathan, distinguishing it from the dominant Three Sisters, named Faith, Hope and Charity by Methodist missionaries.[1] Some late nineteenth-century maps refer to it as the Bachelor, while others variously label it Old Baldy and Snow Mountain.[2] By the early twentieth century, Central Oregonians seem to have settled on the name Bachelor Butte, which is how the feature appeared on early Forest Service maps in the 1920s.

Several years before the ski area opened, an unsigned editorial in Bend's newspaper argued that the feature was "more than a mere butte" and deserved a more dignified title.[3] In 1958, when the ski area opened, the certificate of incorporation referred to the area as the Mt. Bachelor Ski Resort. The belief behind the marketing was that skiers wouldn't be drawn to Bend by the prospect of skiing down a "butte." For that reason, Bill Healy and other backers upgraded its status, though unofficially. Soon after, the Bend Chamber of Commerce began petitioning the Oregon Geographic Names Board to make the name change official.

Lewis L. McArthur, son of Lewis Ankeny "Tam" McArthur, Oregon's foremost authority on geographic place names, noted that "names are dynamic and change with the people and the times."[4] However, in the case of Bachelor Butte, McArthur was somewhat less flexible in his outlook. He believed that the redesignation of Bachelor Butte was an inappropriate concession to "commercial interests" and disrespectful of Oregon's history and tradition.[5]

When it came time to formally consider the matter in the early 1980s, the Oregon Geographic Names Board was divided over the name change. However, the ski area's growing popularity made the decision a virtual fait accompli. Over McArthur's opposition, the board forwarded its recommendation for renaming Bachelor Butte to the United States Board of Geographic Names, which voted to confirm the new designation in October 1983. Henceforth, the "butte" was officially designated a mountain on all federal maps.

For this book, the term Bachelor Butte refers to the geographic feature before the official name change in 1983. After that period, the name Mount Bachelor is generally applied. The stylized term Mt. Bachelor refers specifically to Mt. Bachelor Inc. and the associated ski area.

ACKNOWLEDGEMENTS

Writing history is like assembling a puzzle when many people hold the pieces. Putting together the picture requires finding those who can help locate its various parts. During my attempt to tell Mount Bachelor's history, numerous individuals generously offered their recollections, documents and photographs, helping piece together the puzzle.

First and foremost, credit must go to the late Peggy Chessman Lucas, author of *Mt. Bachelor: Bill Healy's Dream*. Lucas was a fifth-generation Oregonian, born in Pendleton and raised in Astoria. In 1936, she graduated from the University of Oregon's School of Journalism and later worked as a freelance writer for Gannett newspapers and the *Oregonian*. In 1974, she moved to Central Oregon and lived at Black Butte Ranch, where she edited the monthly newsletter and authored a book about the community's history.

Toward the end of his life, Bill Healy asked Lucas to write a history of Mt. Bachelor's establishment. Lucas interviewed many members of the founding generation and captured the story of how the resort came to be. Sadly, Healy died before Lucas completed the manuscript. Had she not accepted the project when she did, much of that story would have been lost to history.

Several local historians have done exceptional work adding to that story. Les Joslin is the author of numerous books about Central Oregon history and the U.S. Forest Service. He provided enormous assistance on various topics, including the Deschutes National Forest.

Steve Stenkamp is another passionate historian and former mayor of Bend. He is an undisputed expert on Oregon's lost ski areas and has endless knowledge of Mt. Bachelor from his many years of working and skiing on the mountain. Steve was incredibly generous with his time, helping locate documents and photographs in the Deschutes County Historical Society archives. He was also the source for much of the lift chronology, which was supplemented by data from the Forest Service.

Tor Hanson, a native of Sweden, moved to Bend in the early 1990s and made important contributions chronicling the early Scandinavian migration to Bend and development of the logging industry. He was extremely helpful with the chapters about the histories of the Skyline Ski Club, the Sunriver resort and Bend's early ski culture.

A great deal of the information in this book came from the archives of our local newspaper, the *Bulletin*. Since 1903, its staff has done invaluable reporting on topics important to Central Oregonians, including Mount Bachelor. Similarly, the Deschutes County Historical Society was an invaluable source for articles, documents and photographs. Special thanks to the museum manager, Vanessa Ivey, for her help with reproducing many of the images used in the book.

Many other individuals generously provided their time and recollections helping with this research. Jane Meissner shared stories of her parents' years running the ski school at Mt. Bachelor and their significant contributions to Central Oregon's ski culture. John Schiemer, Molly Cogswell-Kelley, Frank Cammack, Howard Friedman and Coggin Hill provided interviews and pictures about the Mt. Bachelor Sports Education Foundation and its athletes.

Bob Mathews, Bob Woodward and Dennis Oliphant offered recollections and documents relating to the early history of Mt. Bachelor's Nordic Center. Diane Armpriest helped track down her master's thesis on landscape architecture focused on the early development of the Nordic Center. Jay Bowerman and Rich Gross helped piece together the intermittent history of the biathlon program and shooting ranges around Mount Bachelor.

Rick Schafer was incredibly generous in offering several rare photographs taken by his stepfather and mentor, Ray Atkeson, during his trips to Mount Bachelor. Rick Wesseler of the Deschutes National Forest offered invaluable assistance concerning Mt. Bachelor's relationship with the U.S. Forest Service, as did Jillian Gantt with archival images. Mathew Brock of the Mazama Library and Jeff Thomas provided background information concerning Mount Bachelor's early climbing history.

Dr. Dan Jaffe, professor of atmospheric and environmental chemistry at the University of Washington, provided information about his team's crucial scientific work at the Mount Bachelor Observatory. Dr. David Lewis, assistant professor at Oregon State University, provided background research on Oregon's tribal treaties and assistance with the land acknowledgement.

Numerous individuals and organizations provided images used in this book, including the Deschutes County Historical Society, the Mazama Library, the Deschutes National Forest, the Ray Atkeson Image Archive, the Colorado Snowsports Museum and Hall of Fame, the Tucker Sno-Cat Corporation, the Mt. Bachelor Sports Education Foundation, Jane Meissner, Steve Stenkamp, Tom Healy, Bob Mathews, LeeAnn Kriegh, Craig Skinner, Tom Iraci, Bob Woodward, the Gillis family and Dan Jaffe, among others.

Many readers reviewed portions of the manuscript and graciously provided suggestions to improve the book. These included Les Joslin, Tor Hanson, Steve Stenkamp, Bob Mathews, LeeAnn Kriegh, Tom Healy, Dave Rathbun, Tom Lomax and Susan Conrad.

Special thanks to Bend author Sara Rishforth for helping with the book proposal and to Roundabout Books for their ongoing support of Bend authors and readers. Thanks to Johnny Sereni at Mt. Bachelor for his support and help with the cover design. I would like to thank Laurie Krill, acquisitions editor at Arcadia, who provided support for the book concept and helped bring it into print.

INTRODUCTION

Mount Bachelor is one of Central Oregon's more recognizable landmarks and an important part of the region's history, economy and culture. But the mountain's history is about far more than a ski resort. It tells an important story about changing values and our evolving relationship with the natural environment.

The region's Indigenous tribes relied on this land for basic subsistence: hunting, gathering plants and collecting volcanic obsidian for tools and trade. Their culture was well adapted to Central Oregon's ecosystem, with patterns of life defined by seasonal movements based on the availability of resources. Their nomadic lifestyle left little lasting impact except for a few faded pictographs and archaeological remnants of scattered campsites around the high lakes and along the banks of the Deschutes River.

During the mid-nineteenth century, the arrival of Euro-American settlers fundamentally altered the relationship between humans and the land. At first, their subsistence involved relatively low-impact activities centered on small-scale farming and animal husbandry. But gradually, settlers pushed higher into the mountains seeking alpine pastures for grazing their livestock and pristine forests for hunting and recreation.

The railroad's arrival in the early twentieth century brought about a dramatic transformation in how the land was valued and used by local inhabitants. Westward expansion created an enormous demand for timber, and Central Oregon became one of the nation's largest producers of pine. Sawmills along the Deschutes River became the lifeblood of the local economy and permanently altered the region's landscape and culture.

For several decades, logging companies clear-cut millions of acres of mostly private timber holdings in the Deschutes basin, the Paulina Mountains and west into the Cascade foothills. The logging industry brought waves of new arrivals, including many immigrants from Scandinavia. These men and women became Central Oregon's early ski pioneers, combining a traditional affinity for winter sports with an environment that was well suited to outdoor recreation.

By the early 1950s, timber production plateaued as resources dwindled and the margins for lumber shrank. Slowing economic growth brought about another change in how Central Oregonians viewed and valued the natural landscape. This change involved transitioning away from an economy built on commodity extraction toward a different model based on conservation and outdoor recreation. Mount Bachelor and the surrounding Deschutes National Forest played a critical role in this next evolution.

Several factors helped turn a dying logging town into a regional hub for outdoor recreation and tourism. Bill Healy, Mt. Bachelor's founder, brought the vision and ambition for turning Bachelor Butte into a major North American ski resort. Perhaps his most important quality was his ability to generate enthusiasm and support from the local community. Without this, his dream of developing the ski area might never have become a reality.

Early in the process, Healy and his backers made several important decisions that profoundly impacted the course of the region's development. The first of these concerned matters of timing and location. Healy had detailed knowledge of the local area and chose an ideal place to establish a winter resort. He did this when only a handful of other ski areas were operating around the state.

Healy also understood that Mt. Bachelor could not survive by relying solely on local skiers. Early on, he and the other board members promoted the area to visitors outside Central Oregon. Soon, the area was drawing guests from across the Pacific Northwest and California for skiing and other winter activities. The resort's popularity with non-locals provided the critical financial foundation for developing Bend's fledgling tourism economy.

One critical juncture was Healy's decision to forego slope-side development around the mountain. After a brief experiment with on-site lodging in the late 1960s, Healy abandoned the effort and decided that Mt. Bachelor would remain a day-use resort. This helped spur growth in nearby Bend and Sunriver, making these areas partners rather than competitors in the burgeoning tourism economy. This decision preserved much of the unspoiled natural environment around Mount Bachelor that was lost in other resort communities pursuing different development priorities.

Another example of Healy's forward-thinking vision was his determination to expand the skiable terrain to Mount Bachelor's summit. This reflected a desire to fully realize the mountain's enormous potential and enable the resort to distinguish itself from competing ski areas. That vision ultimately elevated Mt. Bachelor into a nationally known ski destination rather than limiting its appeal to a smaller, regional audience.

A final factor in Healy's success was his talent for engaging local stakeholders, including a long and productive collaboration with the U.S. Forest Service. Such a partnership was not necessarily the norm for all ski resorts operating on national forest lands. However, Healy and subsequent leaders generally made the relationship work to the benefit of residents and the economy while also protecting the invaluable natural resources of the Deschutes National Forest.

The evolving relationship between people and the land is a central theme of this story. At times, it involved conflicting goals when conservation was sacrificed for economic development. But as the region's economy transformed, so did values regarding how to best use and protect the land. Preservation and sustainability became higher priorities as outdoor recreation emerged as an important source of the region's economic growth and prosperity.

Today, Central Oregon faces new challenges in balancing a desire for conservation against the negative effects of development. These concerns are exacerbated by the pressures of climate change and rapid population growth. While tourism and recreation have helped preserve our treasured natural spaces, they have also contributed to their degradation. These issues demand new thinking and compromises to sustain prosperity while also protecting the natural spaces that make Central Oregon a unique place to live.

CHAPTER 1

BACHELOR BUTTE:
A NATURAL AND CULTURAL HISTORY

GEOPHYSICAL OVERVIEW

Mount Bachelor and the surrounding Cascade Range are defined by a history of volcanism related to the Cascadia Subduction Zone. The term *subduction zone* refers to the convergence line between tectonic plates off the Oregon coast where the Juan de Fuca Plate sinks under the North American Plate.[6] Movement of the plates generates earthquakes around the subduction zone and magmatism (the motion of magma) parallel to the convergent boundaries. The line of magmatism from the Cascadia Subduction Zone extends from northern California to British Columbia, with volcanos as the surface expression of this phenomenon. Central Oregon has several large volcanos that are part of this chain.

From a geologic perspective, the Cascades can be divided into two distinct parts: the Western Cascades and the High Cascades. The Western Cascades experienced an earlier period of volcanic activity due to the gradual eastward movement of the subduction zone. Much of the visible evidence from that period has been erased by erosion and covered with dense vegetation. Conversely, the High Cascades, including Mount Bachelor and the Three Sisters region, experienced a later period of volcanic activity as the subduction zone shifted. Today, the volcanos of the older Western Cascades are extinct, while those of the younger High Cascades remain active.

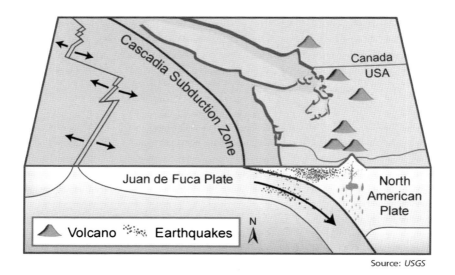

Source: *USGS*

Cascadia Subduction Zone. *U.S. Geological Survey.*

Several volcano types are found in Central Oregon, including shield volcanos, cinder cones and composite volcanos. Shield volcanoes have a lower profile with more gentle slopes due to highly fluid lava moving over an extended period. The steady accumulation of lava gives these volcanoes their distinct shield-like shape. Shield volcanos often have cave-like lava tubes and cinder cones around their base. The Newberry Caldera to the east of Mount Bachelor is an example of a shield volcano.

Cinder cones are steep hills of cinders or ash ejected from a central vent. These cones are often symmetrical and rounded at the bottom, with uniform slopes between thirty and forty degrees. They frequently have bowl-shaped craters at the summit and are found around the flanks of shield volcanoes, stratovolcanoes and calderas. There are dozens of cinder cones scattered throughout the Central Oregon Cascades, including the prominent Egan Cone adjacent to Mount Bachelor's north slope.

Several composite volcanoes (also known as stratovolcanoes) are present around Mount Bachelor. These are cone-shaped volcanoes formed by viscous (slow-moving) lava, pumice and volcanic ash layers. They tend to form taller peaks and may consist of two or more volcanoes in the same formation. Examples of this volcano type include South Sister, Middle Sister and Broken Top.

Mount Bachelor is a stratovolcano sitting atop a shield volcano. It is part of the Mount Bachelor Volcanic Chain, formed around twelve thousand years ago. The entire chain is visible from Mount Bachelor's summit, extending along a southern trend line as far as Lookout Mountain, to the east of Crane Prairie Reservoir. Mount Bachelor sits at the north end of this twenty-five-kilometer chain that includes numerous cinder cones, lava flows and shield volcanoes.

Scattered around Mount Bachelor's summit are vents that once discharged lava, including several located near the lift terminal building. The vents appear as low, irregularly shaped domes and shallow collapsed craters; however, there is presently no geothermal activity on the mountain. Several smaller pyroclastic cones (cinder cones or scoria cones) are visible around the summit.[7] A cluster of vents and plugs extends to the top of the northeast-facing glacial cirque. At several locations around the mountain, one can see evidence of old lava flows, including two lava tubes known as the Dutchman Caves located near the bottom of the Rainbow lift.

Mount Bachelor formed over several discrete eruptive periods, starting as early as 12,500 years ago. The summit formation was probably completed

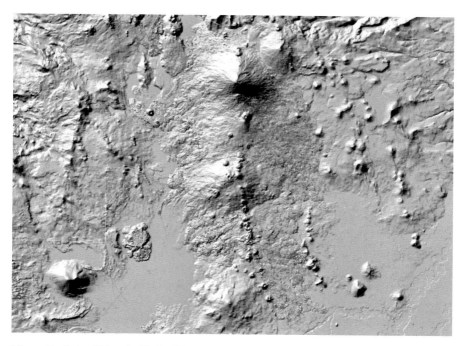

Mount Bachelor Volcanic Chain, lidar image. *U.S. Geological Survey.*

Aerial view of the Three Sisters. *Left to right*: South Sister, Middle Sister and North Sister. The rhyolite lava flow in the foreground is approximately 2,200 years old. *Photograph by Lyn Topinka. U.S. Geological Survey.*

around 10,000 years ago, making Mount Bachelor the youngest of the major volcanos in the Three Sisters region.[8] The volcano's last active period occurred around 2,000 years later, before the eruption of Mount Mazama, which formed the Crater Lake caldera. Mount Bachelor's last active period produced lava flows on the mountain's north flank and formed the large scoria cone, informally known as Egan Cone, adjacent to the West Village base area. According to the U.S. Geological Survey, future eruptive activity on Mount Bachelor is unlikely.[9]

Mount Bachelor's summit offers a dramatic overview of the region's volcanic legacy. The Newberry Volcano is visible directly to the southeast, and the Mount Bachelor Volcanic Chain extends to the south. The Three Sisters and Broken Top dominate the horizon to the north. Beyond that are Mount Jefferson, Mount Hood and Mount Adams. On a clear day, it's possible to see Mount Shasta, an enormous steep-sided stratovolcano some 180 miles to the south in Northern California.

GLACIAL HISTORY

Central Oregon's glaciers have been a subject of scientific interest since the beginning of Euro-American settlement. In 1858, Dr. John Strong Newberry, a physician and naturalist with the U.S. Army survey expedition, was the first scientist to document evidence of glacial action in the Three Sisters region. In 1903, the noted geologist and geographer Israel Cook Russell visited the region and took some of the earliest photographs of the area's glaciers. His research was the first to substantiate the evidence of glacial recession in the Three Sisters region.[10]

Cascade glaciers have been retreating since the end of the last ice age, around ten thousand years ago; however, the loss rate has increased in recent years due to climate change. Snow surveys dating back to the 1950s have identified around thirty named glaciers in the Three Sisters region. Today, only thirteen remain, and several are at risk of vanishing soon, including three on South Sister (North Skinner, Skinner and Carver Glaciers) and two on Broken Top (Crook and Bend Glaciers).[11]

Dutchman Glacier, circa 1938. *Photograph by Kenneth Phillips, courtesy of the Mazama Library.*

Mount Bachelor's era of glacial retreat likely began around the same time as the formation of the Mount Bachelor Volcanic Chain in the late Pleistocene epoch, around twelve thousand years ago.[12] For this reason, Mount Bachelor has few areas of glacial erosion except for the cirque on the north slope just below the summit. That cirque extends down to a terminal moraine, impounding a small lake just above mid-mountain.

The Dutchman Glacier once occupied the cirque on the north slope. In 1938, Kenneth Phillips, head of the Mazamas' Research Committee, led a detailed study of the region's glacial shrinkage, taking photographs and documenting the Dutchman Glacier's retreat.[13] As part of that study, Phillips took what may have been the last known pictures of the Dutchman Glacier before it disappeared sometime in the 1940s. Today, Crook Glacier on Broken Top is Oregon's southernmost remaining glacier.[14]

CLIMATE AND WEATHER

Proximity to the Pacific Ocean and the Coastal Range defines the climate patterns of the High Cascades. Areas to the west of the range enjoy a temperate maritime climate. Moist air from the ocean rises and cools as it moves to the east over the foothills. In the wintertime, this generates significant snowfall in the mountains. The coldest temperatures occur between December and January, while most snowfall comes between November and March.

Locations on the western slopes of the Cascades receive as much as seventy-five inches of total annual precipitation, deceasing rapidly on the east side of the range. Historic averages at the Dutchman Flat measuring station typically record between fifty-five and sixty inches annually of overall precipitation.[15]

The ski area reports an average snowfall of 462 inches per year at the resort with an average base of 150–200 inches. During the 2010–11 season, the mountain received a record snowfall of 665 inches, surpassing the previous record of 606 inches during the 1998–99 season.[16]

Approximately 80 percent of Mount Bachelor's annual precipitation falls as snow, generating a ski season lasting from the middle of November through the end of May. Mount Bachelor has no named streams, but rain and snowmelt seep directly into the porous volcanic rock and eventually emerge as groundwater flowing into the Deschutes River basin.

It is not uncommon for Mount Bachelor to experience 60 to 70 mph winds during storm cycles. Winds as high as 200 mph have been recorded on Mount Bachelor's 9,065-foot summit. Temperatures in the area range significantly between seasons, sometimes reaching 90° F in the summer to as low as −20° F in the winter. Conditions can change rapidly in any season.

THE CENTRAL CASCADES ECOREGION

Mount Bachelor is one of twenty peaks over a height of seven thousand feet within the 1.6-million-acre Deschutes National Forest. The forest includes several unique habitats supporting more than three hundred fish and wildlife species.[17] It contains more than 150 lakes and five hundred miles of rivers and streams encompassing several distinct ecoregions.

Much of the region surrounding Mount Bachelor is classified as Cascade Crest Montane Forest ecoregion, an undulating plateau of volcanic buttes and cones reaching about 6,500 feet. This region contains many glaciated lakes and is heavily forested. Mount Bachelor itself falls within the Cascades Subalpine/Alpine ecoregion. This is an area of glaciated volcanic peaks rising above subalpine meadows over 6,500 feet. It contains numerous cascading streams, glacial cirques and tarns excavated by glacial movement.

The Deschutes River is the region's main waterway. Originating high in the Cascades, it provides much of the water for the eastern side of the mountains. The river's headwaters form at Little Lava Lake, near Mount Bachelor's southwest base. It is fed by springs along its banks and flows southward into Crane Prairie Reservoir, then into Wickiup Reservoir, where much of the water is stored and released as needed for seasonal irrigation and instream uses. After leaving Wickiup Reservoir, the Deschutes turns northeasterly, flowing past Sunriver and through Bend. Around 90 percent of the river's flow is diverted into canals during the summer months to support agricultural irrigation.

FLORA

A combination of elevation, moisture, wind and soil type determines the vegetation patterns in the High Cascades. Flora is adapted to cold temperatures, a short growing season and deep snow. On Mount Bachelor, the natural timberline ranges between 7,200 and 7,600 feet, roughly at mid-mountain.

Mountain hemlock is the most prevalent tree found around Mount Bachelor, growing up to 150 feet tall with a diameter of three feet. The

Mountain hemlocks in the Three Sisters Wilderness. *U.S. Forest Service.*

hemlock's cones are around three inches long, with needles of blue-green color, less than an inch long. The tree thrives in harsh conditions and has a relatively short growing season. It's often found in areas with significant snow accumulation. The trees' crowns and branches are frequently covered with lichens in the stands around Mount Bachelor.

Lodgepole pines are found at a lower elevation on the southeast and northern aspects of the mountain, where they thrive in the cold temperatures. They are associated with ash and pumice deposits and often appear in densely crowded stands, especially in burn areas. These distinctive, two-needle pines grow thin and straight. They have thin bark, making them susceptible to fire, wind and insects. Periodic burns allow this fire-dependent species to regenerate and maintain its niche in the ecosystem.

At higher elevations are pockets of scrubby whitebark pine, Central Oregon's highest-elevation tree species. Whitebark pines can tolerate poor soils and harsh weather conditions higher on the mountain where other trees can't survive. They play an essential role in retaining moisture and countering erosion. On Mount Bachelor, the heaviest concentrations of whitebark pine are located on the southern and southeastern aspects. Weather-beaten

Whitebark pine in the Cascades. *Photograph by Richard Sniezko, U.S. Forest Service.*

whitebark pines are also found around the top of nearby Tumalo Mountain, a popular destination for hikers and backcountry skiers.

Whitebark pines are dependent on Clark's nutcrackers for reproduction. The birds bury the seeds for winter, and some of those eventually develop into seedlings. Whitebark pines grow up to fifty feet tall and two feet in diameter. They have short, stiff needles that grow in bundles of five, distinguishing them from lodgepole pines, which have two needles per bundle. The species has been devastated in recent years due to fungal disease, bark beetles and climate change. It was recently designated as a threatened species by the U.S. Fish and Wildlife Service, making it eligible for special protection under the Endangered Species Act.

Volcanic rock and sparse vegetation characterize the areas above Mount Bachelor's tree line. Low soil moisture, wind exposure and poor soil fertility limit vegetation in this zone. However, plants and ground cover are essential for stabilizing the rocky volcanic soil, and a variety of wildflowers can be found on the mountain's slopes during the summertime.

Western pasqueflowers are perennial wildflowers common in alpine and subalpine meadows. They appear in meadows and sandy mountain slopes

Western pasqueflowers.
*Photograph by Jason
Hollinger.*

around the tree line as the snow melts. Early in the season, they arrive as large, cream-colored blossoms. The petals drop after the initial bloom, turning into spiky green balls. Late in the season, they become a fluffy mass of seeds resembling white hair.

The mountain's rocky outcroppings support Davidson's penstemon, which grows in short, dense mats, two to five inches tall. Each plant has one flower per stem with five sepals of white or purplish color. Davidson's penstemon blooms in early summer, just after the snow disappears in alpine areas. Indian paintbrush is also common around Mount Bachelor and blooms from late spring to midsummer. It is a perennial herb that does well in sandy, well-drained soils. Indian paintbrush grows between one and three feet tall with a distinctive bright red color.

Other plants found around Mount Bachelor include pussy paws and partridge foot. Pussy paws are small, succulent flowering plants with brightly colored flowers. Their reddish or pink flowers bloom late spring into summer, and they grow low to the ground, thriving in the sandy and pumice soils.

Partridge foot is a mat-forming semi-shrub that grows in barren areas, often above the tree line. It can be found in sandy, subalpine and alpine soils on shaded ground, typically appearing in areas where snow persists late into the season. The flowers are white but may appear yellowish, and each flower has five petals.

Spotted saxifrage grows in a moss-like cushion, two to six inches high. It has five white petals with distinctive red or purple dots, yellow-orange spots near the base and oblong petals. Spotted saxifrage flowers in late spring to early summer, growing in rocky outcrops, scree and crevices in subalpine and alpine areas.

Davidson's penstemon. *Photograph by Walter Siegmund.*

Pussy paw. *Photograph by Jane Shelby Richardson.*

Above, left: Spotted saxifrage. *Photograph by Jacob W. Frank, National Park Service.*

Above, right: Indian paintbrush. *Photograph by Neal Herbert, Yellowstone National Park.*

Left: Pumice grape-fern. *National Park Service.*

The rare and threatened pumice grape-fern can be found on Mount Bachelor's loose volcanic soils. This grayish-green, single-leaf perennial appears at higher elevations after the snowpack recedes in late summer. However, it requires moist conditions and does not always emerge. It has a narrow habitat range, primarily in central and south-central Oregon, with some species found on Shastina, Mount Shasta's secondary cone in Northern California. Its small size and habitat on loose pumice make it vulnerable to damage from recreational activities such as hiking and mountain biking.

FAUNA

Mount Bachelor's forested slopes provide habitats for many wildlife species, including birds, deer, elk and small mammals. Mule deer and black-tailed deer are found around Mount Bachelor during the summer months. Streams and meadows around Todd Creek and Dutchman Creek serve as fawning and calving grounds. Deer forage in open-canopy areas and spaces cleared by fire or timber harvest that offer abundant leafy plants, blackberry, huckleberry and grasses during summer.

In the winter, deer migrate to lower elevations and are often seen on the trails and streets around Bend. Their breeding season usually begins in November and ends in December, with newborns arriving in late spring or early summer. Local mule deer populations have declined significantly over the last twenty years, caused by disease and human disturbance of their habitat from recreation, development and poaching.

Elk can be found in similar habitats as mule deer; however, they generally try to avoid human activity. The elk feed on grasses, herbs, twigs and bark. The animals store body fat during the summer, providing insulation and energy reserves for winter, when their diet consists of lower-nutrient foods such as bitterbrush and sagebrush. Winter fat reserves can be as much as 30 percent of an elk's total body mass.

Black bears, mountain lions, bobcats and coyotes can be found in the area during certain times of the year. Two species of wild cats live within the Deschutes National Forest, the cougar (mountain lion) and the bobcat. Cougars are native to Oregon and are the state's largest felid. They consume mainly deer, elk, raccoons, bighorn sheep and other mammals, often ranging several miles a day to hunt. They are territorial animals, and male cougars

Above: Mule deer. *Oregon Department of Fish and Wildlife.*

Opposite: Yellow-bellied marmot. *Photograph by Patrick Myers, National Park Service.*

have a home range of up to seventy-five miles. They generally avoid people and are rarely seen; however, early morning skiers on the Nordic trails can occasionally spot their tracks in the snow during springtime.

The Deschutes National Forest is home to the black bear. Black bears are typically found in dense forests near water sources. They are omnivorous and will feed on almost anything, including grasses, nuts, berries, honey, fruits, bark, insects and larvae, small mammals and fish. Black bears are shy animals and rarely spotted in areas with human activity.

Bobcats live in the wilderness around Mount Bachelor; however, they are solitary, nocturnal animals and rarely spotted during daytime. Bobcats are not adapted to hunting in deep snow; therefore, they tend to spend the winter at lower elevations. Bobcats generally hunt at dusk and dawn and will eat rabbits, small mammals and birds; they have been known to hunt deer on occasion.

The lodgepole pine stands around the mountain's base provide habitat for American martens. These animals are usually golden brown to dark brown on the feet and tail, with the head somewhat lighter. Martens are active year-round and can catch prey by following tracks in the snow.

Yellow-bellied marmots, also known as rock chucks, live among the boulders, rocky slopes and log piles throughout Central Oregon. The yellow-bellied marmot is the largest member of the squirrel family in Oregon and emerges from hibernation in late winter and early spring.

The American pika, a species related to rabbits and hares, is adapted to cooler temperatures and is found in higher-elevation microhabitats of the Cascades. Pikas typically hide among rock piles and lava flows and can be identified by the distinctive, squeaky chirp they use to defend territory and attract mates.

The Sierra Nevada red fox has been spotted in recent years around Mount Bachelor's Nordic trails. It is one of the rarest and most endangered subspecies of red fox in North America. Before these animals arrived in Central Oregon, conservationists believed that fewer than fifty of them remained in two isolated colonies in the California Sierras. The first sightings in Central Oregon were made in 2012, but the number of foxes in the area is unknown.

Top: Sierra Nevada red fox. *Photo by LeeAnn Kriegh.*

Bottom: Lynx. *Photo by Magnus Johansson.*

Native lynx have been documented in the High Cascades; however, not much is known about the habitat of existing populations. Unlike bobcats, lynx can hunt and thrive at higher elevations in the winter and are well adapted to deep snow. They occupy the mountainous areas near timberline and avoid human activity.

Wolverines have been documented in isolated wilderness habitats in the Deschutes National Forest; however, it is uncertain if any remain. Chipmunks, ground squirrels and various species of rabbits, gophers and mice can be found in abundance and constitute an important food source for larger carnivores.

Many birds make their home in the forests around the mountain. Eagles are permanent residents in the area, often breeding around the Upper Deschutes River and Wickiup Reservoir during late winter. An eagle's wingspan can vary from six to seven feet, and they have exceptional eyesight. They often pair for life and build large, heavy nests measuring up to six feet wide and weighing hundreds of pounds. Eagles have a strong attachment to nesting locations and often return yearly.

Top: Clark's nutcracker. *Photograph by David Menke, U.S. Fish and Wildlife Service.*

Bottom: Pileated woodpecker. *Photograph by Josh Laymon.*

Clark's nutcrackers live among the whitebark pine stands and are critical to the trees' reproduction. Blue grouse can be found in the conifer forests during the winter months. Several species of hawks inhabit the area, including the sharp-shinned hawk, the northern goshawk and the red-tailed hawk. The latter are frequently spotted in the forests around Mount Bachelor's slopes.

Several woodpecker species are found around Mount Bachelor, including the pileated woodpeckers in the older-growth mixed conifer forests. Black-backed woodpeckers occupy the lodgepole pine stands, and three-toed woodpeckers can be found in higher elevations and among the pine stands.

The area is a dispersed habitat for spotted owls, mainly around the northern and western slopes of the mountain. The great gray owl can be found among the mixed conifer forests around the mountain's base. Many other species of birds live in the surrounding woods, including pine siskins, blackbirds, bluebirds, chickadees, crossbills, hummingbirds, jays, juncos, sparrows and ravens.

CULTURAL HISTORY

Humans have lived in Central Oregon for over nine thousand years. Food scarcity and challenging climate conditions meant that the region's early Indigenous inhabitants likely lived in small extended-family groups. They were primarily nomadic, making seasonal rounds for hunting, fishing and gathering wild plants to be stored for the winter. During colder months, small groups typically camped for the season at lower elevations, close to water sources.[18]

The first humans to visit the area around Bachelor Butte were likely bands of Northern Paiute. A few miles to the northwest, near Devil's Lake, archaeologists have found evidence of Indigenous encampments and pictographs. Early climbers of Bachelor Butte and South Sister in the late nineteenth century reported finding large rock cairns and pieces of wood on the summit, suggesting that local tribes had frequented the mountain peaks long before Euro-American settlement.[19]

During development of the Wickiup Reservoir in the 1930s, archaeologists discovered knives made from obsidian (volcanic glass) dating back to the late glacial or post-glacial period, suggesting that humans visited parts of the Upper Deschutes before the eruption of Mount Mazama some 7,700 years ago.[20] Early ranchers who used this area for grazing livestock named it Wikiup after the winter shelters used by the Northern Paiute. These shelters consisted of brush-covered, dome-shaped wooden frames, eight to fourteen feet in diameter.[21]

Few records reveal how Native inhabitants referred to these lands; however, many current landmarks are known by Indigenous names. The prominent Kaleetan Butte, seen on the hike up from Devil's Lake to South Sister, comes from the Chinook word for "arrow." Kwolh Butte, an imposing cinder cone to the south of Mount Bachelor, is named after the Chinook

Indigenous pictograph on a basalt column near Devil's Lake. *Photograph by Craig Skinner.*

Depiction of a Northern Paiute camp and Wikiup shelter with Bachelor Butte in the background. *Artwork by Eugenia "Genie" Waterhouse, courtesy of the Sunriver Nature Center.*

word for "aunt."[22] The name for Wanoga Butte, located off the highway connecting Sunriver to Mount Bachelor, comes from the Klamath word for "son" or "male child." The name for Tumalo Mountain, adjacent to Mount Bachelor, comes from a Klamath word meaning "wild plum."

Euro-American exploration of the area began in the 1820s with the Hudson Bay Company's expedition led by Peter Skene Ogden. His party traveled along the Deschutes River as far as the Crooked River and reported several "lofty mountains" that would most likely have been the Three Sisters and Bachelor Butte.[23] A second Ogden team later traversed the Paulina Mountains south of Bend.

As settlers occupied the Willamette Valley in the 1840s, parties began exploring the High Cascades from the west. Captain John Fremont's expedition of 1843 included Thomas "Broken Hand" Fitzpatrick, who allegedly gave his name to the ridgeline extending east from the Broken Top plateau. An 1855 Pacific Railroad Survey, led by Lieutenant Henry Larcom Abbot of the U.S. Army Corps of Topographical Engineers, surveyed the Upper Deschutes Basin and the high lakes region. The following year, the

Preston sectional map of Oregon and Washington was the first map to depict the Three Sisters; however, Mount Bachelor and the lesser peaks did not appear on that version.

Shortly after Oregon achieved statehood in 1859, Euro-American settlers began moving into Central Oregon. In 1862, Felix Scott, Marion Scott, John Craig and Robert Millican became the first settlers to winter in the area, bringing nine hundred head of cattle with them. Settlement in the Deschutes Basin began in earnest in the 1870s, with early economic activity focused on farming, ranching and raising livestock, especially sheep.

In the early 1890s, William P. Vandevert arrived from the Willamette Valley and settled on the Little Deschutes River, near the present-day site of Sunriver. Vandevert was a renowned hunter and served as one of the first forest rangers in Central Oregon.[24] The family's original homestead operated for nearly one hundred years before being converted into a residential community still known as Vandevert Ranch, located south of Sunriver.

Judge John Breckenridge Waldo and Adolph Dekum may have been the first Euro-Americans to summit Bachelor Butte, in the summer of 1883. However, they were likely not the first persons to visit the top. Waldo was an avid outdoorsman and Oregon Supreme Court chief justice.[25] During the 1880s, he traveled extensively by horseback along much of the Cascade crest between Mount Jefferson and Mount Shasta. During that time, Waldo kept detailed notes of his travels.[26]

In early September 1883, the men camped in the vicinity of Lava Lake and noted what they described as the Eastern, Northern and Western Sisters, likely referring to Bachelor Butte, Broken Top and South Sister, given their perspective.

On September 9, Dekum wrote that they had summited the "easternmost" Sister, most likely Bachelor Butte, located a few miles north of their campsite. During the climbs, Dekum was often confused about the party's location and wrote of being "at a loss which of the five peaks are the Three Sisters."[27] The men were able to reorient several days later while summiting South Sister, which Dekum referred to as the "western sister" in his diary entries.[28]

The men climbed South Sister along the southeast ridge starting from Green Lakes, and from the summit, they were able to identify their previous route up Bachelor Butte. During the climbs, Waldo and Dekum noted the presence of rock cairns several feet high, which "seemed to have been piled up by human hands."[29] Dekum also found pieces of flint and wood slivers in a hole, indicating that Native Americans had likely visited both summits long before the start of Euro-American settlement.[30]

Judge John Breckenridge Waldo, Oregon Supreme Court chief justice and likely the first Euro-American to summit Bachelor Butte, in early September 1883. *Oregon Historical Society.*

Judge Waldo is often referred to as "Oregon's John Muir" and was an early proponent of conservation in the High Cascades. Along with William Gladstone Steel, founder of the Mazamas, Waldo became a leading force in persuading President Grover Cleveland to proclaim Oregon's first federal forest reserve in 1893 and later lobbied for the creation of the national park at Crater Lake. Waldo Lake, near Willamette Pass, is named in his honor.

LOGGING AND RECREATION
IN THE DESCHUTES NATIONAL FOREST

By the early twentieth century, Central Oregon's economy began shifting to agriculture and logging. The first commercial sawmill was established in 1901. Shortly after that, the city of Bend was incorporated in 1905 with around five hundred residents. The prospects for development changed dramatically in 1911 when commercial rail service reached Bend via the Great Northern Railroad Oregon Trunk Line. Within a decade, logging would become the primary driver of economic development in the region, bringing the first wave of Scandinavian immigrants to Central Oregon.

During the early settlement period, little attention was given to land management. Forest administration was primarily custodial, without the benefit of professional foresters or scientific management. Before the Forest Service's establishment in 1905, a handful of rangers, employed by the General Land Office, was responsible for administering a vast expanse of public lands across Central Oregon. At the same time, population growth and economic development were bringing about dramatic changes to the landscape.[31]

The Forest Homestead Act of 1906 opened forest lands with agricultural potential to homesteaders, drawing settlers to ranch and farm on the newly available land.[32] They began pushing into the high alpine pastures to graze cattle and sheep during summertime. Meanwhile, new logging roads offered greater access for venturing into the Upper Deschutes basin for hunting, fishing and camping.

Concerns about exploitation of natural resources gradually led the federal government to become more involved in resource management to ensure the future productivity of forest lands. In 1893, President Grover Cleveland created the Cascade Range Forest Reserve under the terms of the Forest Service Act. This action withdrew over four million acres of land from the public domain, including the area surrounding Bachelor Butte.

The new authorities granted to the General Land Office under the Forest Service Act were primarily used to promote timber production and watershed protection. In 1905, administration of the reserve was transferred to the newly established U.S. Forest Service under the Department of Agriculture, and the lands were redesignated as national forests.[33] In 1908, the Deschutes National Forest was created from parts of the Blue Mountain, Cascade and Fremont National Forests.

Before the creation of the Deschutes National Forest, large sections of Central Oregon's timberlands had been transferred to private hands, sometimes

Sheep grazing near Sparks Lake with Bachelor Butte in the background, early twentieth century. *Deschutes County Historical Society.*

through questionable means under laws intended to encourage individual homesteading.[34] When the railroad reached Bend in 1911, these timberlands became extremely valuable. Many owners transferred their holdings to middlemen and speculators who later sold them to large logging enterprises.[35] Two Minnesota-based lumber firms, Brooks-Scanlon and Shevlin-Hixon, acquired many of these private claims to the south and east of Bend.

In 1915, these companies established mills on either side of the Deschutes River and began clear-cutting hundreds of thousands of acres, dramatically altering Central Oregon's landscape.[36] The mills were soon the largest timber operations in Oregon. Each one employed around six hundred workers and twice as many loggers.[37] At peak production, they processed more than five hundred million board feet of timber annually. As one historian noted, the mills "brought wealth to some and jobs to thousands."[38]

Bend's economy boomed because of the mills, but the source of that new newfound prosperity rapidly dwindled. Timber companies largely treated ponderosa pine as a "one-time crop" with little concern for conservation and sustaining future yield.[39] The available timber from private landholdings was largely exhausted within a decade. But under the terms of the General Exchange Act of 1922, the companies were permitted to transfer cutover private lands to the national forest in exchange for the right to cut unharvested timber inside the national forest under Forest Service supervision.

Brooks-Scanlon and Shevlin-Hixon mills along the Deschutes River. *Deschutes County Historical Society.*

These exchanges gradually brought cutover lands under Forest Service supervision, enabling improved land management and reforestation. Approximately one-quarter of the land area within the present-day Deschutes National Forest was acquired through such exchanges. This included the area stretching from Lava Butte to the Newberry Caldera, which was almost entirely cleared of old-growth trees by midcentury.

As Bend's population exploded, Bachelor Butte and the surrounding wilderness became popular destinations for recreation. In 1910, Oregon's famed mountaineering club, the Mazamas, made its annual encampment in the Three Sisters region. During that trip, club members summited Bachelor Butte and left a record box and registry at the top.[40] During that same encampment, club member H.H. Prouty made the first verified summit of North Sister, Central Oregon's last unclimbed peak.

In the early 1920s, a primitive wagon road was constructed roughly along the present route of the Cascade Lakes Highway. The new road provided improved access as people began exploring the national forest by car. In 1921, the Forest Service issued a permit to build the Elk Lake Lodge, offering cabins and tents for camping during summertime. By the late 1920s, outdoor clubs such as the Mazamas, Bend's Skyliners and the Obsidians of Eugene were sponsoring weekend hiking trips, cross-country ski tours and climbing excursions into the High Cascades.

The Forest Service established a fire lookout station on Bachelor Butte in the early 1920s, part of a network of lookouts throughout the Deschutes National Forest. Materials for the lookout were carried by packhorse to the summit. When completed, the station was the second-highest fire lookout in Oregon, after the one on Mount Hood. By 1922, the station was linked by a telephone line to the guard post at Elk Lake and eventually to the forest headquarters in Bend.[41]

J.B. Gauldin supervised the final construction of the lookout and became the first seasonal fire guard stationed on Bachelor Butte. During the 1924 season, Shasta Lela Hoover staffed the lookout, becoming one of the first women ever to serve in a Forest Service field position. Hoover, originally from Portland, was a stenographer in Bend's Red Cross office and an aspiring poet. She had previously spent a season at the lookout station on Pine Mountain.[42] Hoover reportedly relished the solitude and was undeterred by the harsh weather conditions on the summit.

Skyliners club hike to the summit of Bachelor Butte, July 1929. Identified in the photo are Chris Kostol, Nels Skjersaa and Robert Sawyer, editor of the *Bend Bulletin*. *Photograph by Paul Hosmer, courtesy of the Mazama Library.*

By the 1920s, hiking Bachelor Butte had become a popular excursion for Bend locals, though it was not without hazards. The fire guards assigned to the station often had to break through snow and ice to open the cabin at the beginning of the season. Summer snowstorms created difficulties for replenishing supplies and maintaining the phone line. Fire guards reported poor visibility, freezing conditions, lightning strikes, rodent infestations and even a bear ascending the summit trail. In 1933, a researcher working for the U.S. Coast and Geodetic Survey became trapped on the summit during an early-season blizzard and had to be rescued several days later.

Due to wear and tear caused by the harsh weather conditions, the original summit station had to be rebuilt in 1931. In 1934, the Forest Service experimented with using portable radiophone sets to overcome the challenge of maintaining a working phone line up to the summit. The Forest Service even attempted using an airplane to resupply the guard station, but this proved impractical. Given the difficulties of maintaining the site and the frequent poor visibility, the station was eventually closed in the late 1930s.

CHAPTER 2

CENTRAL OREGON'S EARLY SKI CULTURE

B end's cultural transformation began in 1911, the inaugural year of the town's train service. Before that time, Central Oregon was isolated from the rest of the state. Only a few hundred people lived in town, and most made a living from farming or ranching. No large sawmills were operating at the time. But with the new train line linking Bend to the Columbia River, commercial logging suddenly became financially viable.

By the early 1920s, Shevlin-Hixon and Brooks-Scanlon were among the leading producers of timber in the country, generating an enormous demand for labor. Between 1905 and 1915, Bend's population surged tenfold, from five hundred to nearly five thousand. Many new arrivals were of Scandinavian origin, bringing with them a native knowledge of snow travel and a love of winter recreation. Gradually, their enthusiasm for snow sports became ingrained in the local culture.

As early as 1914, a ski club had formed in the community of Crescent, and by the early 1920s, at least one hardware store in Bend was selling skis.[43] Three Norwegians, Nils Wulfsberg, Nels Skjersaa and Chris Kostol, along with a Swede named Emil Nordeen, were among the town's early ski pioneers. The men, known as the "four musketeers of the mountains," were the catalyst in the formation of the Skyliners ski club, introducing winter sports to generations of Central Oregonians.[44]

Of the group, Nils Wulfsberg was perhaps the earliest visionary to recognize the potential for turning Central Oregon into a hub of winter recreation. Wulfsberg arrived in Bend in 1927 as a recent graduate of Oslo

Skyliners founding members Nels Skjersaa, Nils Wulfsberg and Emil Nordeen, circa 1928. *Deschutes County Historical Society.*

University and was an advocate for the Norwegian concept of *friluftsliv*, or "open-air living."[45] Wulfsberg believed that winter sport was essential for a healthy lifestyle, stimulating "energy, courage, and initiative."[46] He advocated for developing winter resorts and promoting "ski carnivals," drawing visitors from across Oregon and nearby states.

Emil Nordeen was another early ski pioneer and promotor of the sport. Nordeen was born in Sweden and settled in Bend in 1920 to work in the timber industry. Before commercial ski equipment was available, Nordeen made his own gear using ponderosa pine planks from the Shevlin-Hixon mill.[47] He was an accomplished mountaineer and skier, famous for winning the forty-two-mile Fort Klamath to Crater Lake ski race multiple times.

Nordeen became close friends with a coworker at Brooks-Scanlon named Nels Skjersaa, who had left Norway and emigrated to America in 1914. Nordeen and Skjersaa were avid outdoor athletes who went on long runs together and skied in the mountains.[48] At Brooks-Scanlon, the pair met Chris Kostol, originally from Norway. Kostol had arrived in Bend after being drafted into the U.S. Army in late 1918; he was discharged the following year. Kostol was another skiing enthusiast and allegedly the first person to sell skis in Bend, handcrafted in his workshop.

The origin story of the Skyliners dates to a legendary rescue attempt in 1927. Two young men from the Dalles, Guy Ferry and Henry Cramer, set out to climb the North Sister and South Sister on Labor Day but were caught by an early-season storm.[49] They met forest ranger Prince Glaze near Frog Camp and informed him of their plan. When the men didn't return several days later, search parties set out to find them.

The Bend contingent of rescuers included Wulfsberg, Nordeen, Skjersaa and Kostol. The group first set out for Frog Camp off the McKenzie Highway. From there, they traveled twelve miles on skis before climbing Middle Sister and North Sister in a single day and then returning to camp. Unfortunately, the search was unsuccessful and officially ended on the nineteenth of September. Two years later, hikers discovered the bodies of Ferry and Cramer near the Chambers Lakes, in the saddle between South Sister and Middle Sister.

Paul Hosmer canoeing with his wife, Janis Hosmer, on Mud Lake, with Bachelor Butte in the background. Mud Lake was renamed Hosmer Lake in 1962. *Deschutes County Historical Society.*

Although the group failed to find the missing climbers, the tragedy became the impetus for the creation of the Skyliners. The "four musketeers of the mountains" were the group's founding members, with a charter to "promote all forms of outdoor recreation, especially hiking, camping, mountain climbing, skiing, snowshoeing, skating, and to assist in the acquisition of geological information concerning the Central Oregon country."[50]

Another early member of the club was Paul Hosmer. He was born in Minnesota and moved to Bend to work for Shevlin-Hixon as a company stenographer. During World War I, Hosmer enlisted in the army and served in France. After returning to Bend, he became the editor of the Brooks-Scanlon company newsletter and was known as a skilled outdoorsman and naturalist.

Hosmer won a contest to give the club its name and received a prize of two dollars for his effort. His choice of "Skyliners" was a nod to the Oregon Skyline Trail, a long-distance route established during the early 1920s. The original trail extended roughly 260 miles from Mount Hood to Crater Lake, passing through what would be designated the Three Sisters Wilderness in 1964. Much of the original route has since been integrated into the Pacific Crest Trail. Hosmer was elected president of the Skyliners in 1929 and reelected the following year, serving from 1929 to 1931.[51] Hosmer Lake, with its spectacular views of Mount Bachelor, was named in his honor in 1962.

THE SKYLINERS CLUB AND WINTER SPORTS IN CENTRAL OREGON

In the late 1920s, the Deschutes National Forest issued the Skyliners a permit to develop a winter recreation area seven miles west of the town of Sisters along the road to McKenzie Pass, connecting Central Oregon to the Willamette Valley. Louis Hill, a Great Northern Railroad executive who owned the land, leased it to the club for one dollar per year. The route snaked through rugged lava flows to an elevation of 5,300 feet. The pass was first summited by automobile in 1910, and the road was gradually improved during the 1920s before becoming the club's ski hill in 1928.[52]

Shortly after the club was established, Nils Wulfsberg died suddenly at age twenty-eight. Reports suggested that he had a heart condition that was exacerbated by the strenuous rescue mission the year before. Although Wulfsberg didn't live to see the club come to fruition, it fully reflected his

Skyliners club members in front of the ski jump at the McKenzie Pass location, circa 1930. *Deschutes County Historical Society.*

vision of bringing *friluftsliv* to Central Oregon by promoting winter sports, hikes and outings into the mountains. The club initially had over three hundred active members, and its facilities at McKenzie Pass included a toboggan run, a ski jump, a slalom course and a small lodge.[53]

As skiing gained popularity, the club soon outgrew its site near McKenzie Pass. With a base elevation of 4,200 feet, the location sometimes suffered from lack of snow and was a long drive from Bend. By the early 1930s, the club began searching for a new site. Paul Hosmer led the search committee that eventually located an ideal spot west of Bend, above the banks of Tumalo Creek.[54]

For the new ski hill, the Skyliners took advantage of the improved wagon road leading from Bend along Tumalo Creek up to the site of a new Forest Service station. Initially, there had been a proposal to continue the road up through Soda Springs to Sparks Lake with the intent of building a resort there; however, the project never progressed.[55] The road along Tumalo Creek provided the Skyliners with access to Swede Ridge, a north-facing slope offering nearly 900 feet of vertical elevation over a run of 3,100 feet.

The club began building a ski lodge at a cost of around $40,000. Amid the Depression, funds came from the Emergency Relief Administration, the Civilian Conservation Corps (CCC) and the Forest Service.[56] A CCC crew helped clear the slopes and created a cross-country loop trail connecting several shelters. The lodge was dedicated in 1936, and Skyliners members held dances and fundraisers to help furnish the interior. The project eventually included a ski tow building, a patrol hut and a waxing area.

On the slopes of Swede Ridge, the club built a downhill course, a ski jump and a slalom course for training. The design of the ski jump was based on the facilities built for the 1932 Winter Olympics at Lake Placid. The club eventually had around one thousand dues-paying members when the entire population of Bend was just over five thousand.[57] The Skyliners' hill drew some of the country's top skiers for competitions and often hosted hundreds of guests for weekend skiing. During that time, members of the Skyliners also served as a local search and rescue unit, performing that function until the early 1960s.

Even as the club was developing the ski area above Tumalo Creek, its members were already exploring the slopes of Bachelor Butte. In June 1935, Skyliners members Nels Skjersaa, Chris Kostol and Ray Babcock reportedly climbed to the summit and skied from the top, marking the first documented ski descent of Bachelor Butte. However, other Skyliners had likely done it before without making the news.[58]

In May 1941, the Skyliners held its first downhill race on the butte, starting at the summit and descending 2,500 feet to the timberline. Bend ski pioneer Olaf Skjersaa, younger brother of Nels, won the event, completing the one-mile course in around one and a half minutes. Skjersaa was a well-known local skier and had opened Bend's first ski shop with his wife, Grace, in 1939. Cliff Blann, Mt. Bachelor's future mountain manager, placed third in the race.[59]

Skiing at Tumalo Creek continued through the 1930s, but activity slowed during World War II. The Skyliners resumed operations after the war in the fall of 1947.[60] During the early 1950s, the club began revitalizing the ski hill by adding a new tow rope, lights for night skiing and buses to bring skiers up from Bend.[61] However, the area's low elevation of 4,700 feet offered only around three months of use each winter, while the number of skiers was outgrowing the facilities.

As early as the mid-1940s, local leaders began discussing the possibility of developing a ski area on Bachelor Butte. In 1946, Skyliners president Phillip Gould told the local Kiwanis Club that Bachelor Butte had the potential to be "one of the greatest skiing areas in the country."[62] City leaders began advocating for creation of a winter resort, but progress was slow.

In 1956, the Union Pacific Railroad surveyed the area to evaluate its potential for development. While a rail line was deemed infeasible, the report noted that the site held great potential as a resort, with "good ski slopes for both beginning and expert skiing amongst beautiful scenery."[63] That same year, the Bend Chamber of Commerce organized a committee to explore the possibility of establishing a ski area on Bachelor Butte.

A major fire in January 1957 at the Skyliners hill on Tumalo Creek provided the catalyst to move the plan forward. The blaze destroyed the tow ropes and several buildings, forcing the club to decide whether it was worthwhile to rebuild the facilities. Due to the high cost of replacement, the Skyliners began considering other options.

The following month, several club members led a formal inspection of Bachelor Butte to assess its suitability. The group traveled to the site through deep snow using a Sno-Cat owned by the Soil Conservation Service. The party was led by Gene Gillis and included Don Peters and Ed Parker from the Forest Service along with a representative from the Bend Chamber of Commerce.[64] On its return, the group reported favorably on the location and noted many advantages over the existing hill above Tumalo Creek.

ACCESSING THE HIGH CASCADES

Early wagon routes leading into the Deschutes National Forest were established long before automobiles became a common sight around Bend. However, these roads were primitive at best. Cars appeared in Central Oregon around 1907 but initially were used more for work than recreation. As car ownership increased, it spurred development of improved roads leading into the mountains. One of the earliest routes began at Shevlin Park and ran parallel to Tumalo Creek up Happy Valley to Crater Creek.

In 1920, work began on a section of road leading from Bend to Sparks Lake roughly along the present route of the Cascade Lakes Highway. The wagon road originally cost $10,000 to build and required thousands of pounds of dynamite to clear a path through the lava rock.[65] The route opened at the end of the summer of 1921 and was known as Century Drive for its one-hundred-mile circular route past Bachelor Butte, Elk Lake and Crane Prairie Reservoir, returning to Bend via the Dalles-California Highway.

Above: Route of Century Drive through Dutchman Flat with South Sister and Broken Top in the background, early 1920s. *Deschutes County Historical Society.*

Opposite: Early driving route up Century Drive to Bachelor Butte, date unknown. *Deschutes County Historical Society.*

The new road was used primarily for accessing summer homes and cabins around Elk Lake during the 1920s. Beyond that, there was limited development on Century Drive until the 1930s, when the Civilian Conservation Corps constructed several basic campsites along the road. The stretch of highway just outside Bend was graded and paved before World War II, while the remaining stretch up to Bachelor Butte was covered with volcanic cinder until 1950.[66]

In the mid-1960s, the highway between Bend and Bachelor Butte was expanded to accommodate increasing wintertime traffic as the ski area gained popularity. When Mt. Bachelor opened, the county road department cleared snow between Bend and the resort with a rotary plow and a grader. However, the equipment was often overwhelmed by large storms, causing the resort to lose weeks of operations during some seasons. In 1966, the Oregon State Highway Department assumed responsibility for clearing the route using its heavy plows.[67] During the first year after the change, the resort was able to operate every day of the season without closure due to heavy snow.

By the 1980s, the entire circuit of Century Drive was finally paved with asphalt, significantly improving access to the surrounding Deschutes National Forest.[68] In 1998, a sixty-six-mile portion of the Cascade Lakes Highway was designated as a National Scenic Byway, making the route eligible for additional funding from the Federal Highway Administration. This funding helped add a welcome center, interpretive stops, trailhead improvements and education programs along the highway. Scenic America, a nonprofit conservation organization, named the Cascade Lakes Highway one of its top ten most scenic drives in the United States.

ESTABLISHING THE SKI AREA AT BACHELOR BUTTE

Between the late 1930s and early 1950s, several ski areas had opened around Oregon, including Timberline Lodge and Ski Bowl at Mount Hood, Warner Canyon, Hoodoo and Willamette Pass. Gene Gillis was one of the leading advocates for adding Bachelor Butte to that list. A native of Bend, Gillis was born into a skiing family. His father, Jere Gillis, was an early member and president of Skyliners during the 1930s. Gene was an exceptional all-around athlete, skiing and playing football, basketball, track and field, tennis and golf in high school and, later, football at the University of Oregon.[69]

After joining the Marines and serving in World War II, Gillis earned a spot on the 1948 U.S. Olympic Ski Team; however, he didn't race at the competition in St. Moritz due to an injury sustained during a training run. When his racing career ended, Gillis returned to Central Oregon. In the mid-1950s, he coached junior skiers around Bend and at the Hoodoo ski area, which had opened in 1938 on Santiam Pass.

Gillis had climbed and skied on Bachelor Butte numerous times and was familiar with the area. He had even surveyed it by helicopter for a bird's-eye view of the terrain. In the spring of 1957, Gillis led a small group of skiers to the butte, hoping to convince them of the area's potential. Among the group was Gillis's friend, Bill Healy, a local businessman and active member of the Skyliners club.

Healy was born in Portland and moved to Bend in the 1950s to run his family's furniture business. During World War II, he served in the famed Tenth Mountain Division during combat operations in Italy. After moving to Bend, he became active with the Skyliners.[70] Gillis had convinced Healy of the enormous potential for developing a ski area at Bachelor Butte,

Gene Gillis skiing on Bachelor Butte, circa 1947. *Courtesy of the Gillis family.*

and together, the two became the driving force in selecting the site and establishing the resort.

Several officials from the Deschutes National Forest played an essential role in moving the project forward. James Egan, the forest supervisor, led a group up the snow-covered highway to scout the location on behalf of the Forest Service. After touring the site, he felt that Bachelor Butte would offer a "thrilling location for a winter sports center, with its fine snow and its grand view of the Cascades."[71]

Healy and Gillis organized a group of investors with support from the Bend Chamber of Commerce. Gillis was well connected with other ski resort investors throughout the West and initially went to California seeking outside financing. However, Healy was convinced that the initial sum could be raised locally and began organizing investors from Central Oregon.[72]

Raising money for a new ski area in a town of only twelve thousand residents was an audacious bet, particularly given that Central Oregon was undergoing a painful economic transition. By the early 1950s, the logging industry was suffering from years of overcutting, dwindling profits and industry consolidation.

Brooks-Scanlon purchased Shevlin-Hixon and closed its mill in early 1950, resulting in the loss of around one thousand local jobs.[73] Bend's early ski pioneers, Emil Nordeen and Nels Skjersaa, marked the symbolic end of an era by loading the last railroad car leaving the Shevlin-Hixon mill.[74] Although Brooks-Scanlon continued to operate its mill into the 1990s, the company gradually transitioned from timber production into property development as the logging industry collapsed.

Healy and other local business leaders understood that logging would no longer sustain Central Oregon's economic future. Tourism offered one means of transitioning to a different source of growth. However, the region didn't have the infrastructure or attractions to support year-round tourism. The season generally ran from summer through early fall, with few activities drawing visitors over the mountains during winter.

With characteristic enthusiasm, Healy organized a group of local investors to provide start-up funding for the ski area. The principal investors included Dr. Bradford Pease, Phillip Gould, Felix Marcoulier and Oscar Murray. However, Healy's plan to raise the rest of the money from within the community proved challenging.[75] Some local businessmen and hotel owners were skeptical that the resort would draw many visitors to Bend. Furthermore, when Healy pitched the initial share offering, he stipulated that the investment was for "civic interest," without the expectation of making a profit.[76]

At the time, Paul Hosmer was still serving as editor of the Brooks-Scanlon newsletter and wrote an editorial in support of the project. Healy and his backers eventually convinced another 180 investors to purchase two thousand shares at twenty-five dollars each, raising the remaining portion needed to cover the initial start-up costs.[77] Nearly the entire sum was raised locally. With funding secured, Mt. Bachelor Inc. was incorporated in late July 1957. The board included Bill Healy as president, Phillip Gould as vice president, Dr. Bradford Pease as treasurer and Richard Hickok as secretary.

During the initial planning phase, Healy personally oversaw much of the work with the help of Gene Gillis. Equally important was the assistance of Don Peters, the Deschutes National Forest staff officer responsible for recreation. Peters was a relative newcomer to Bend, arriving from Portland in 1956, but he had considerable firsthand experience managing safety and permitting for other ski resorts in the Pacific Northwest. During a previous assignment in Lakeview, Oregon, he had helped develop Warner Canyon Ski Area, which opened in 1938.

Peters had served as vice president of the Skyliners club when Healy was president and had been among the group that initially recommended Bachelor Butte as the replacement site for the old ski hill above Tumalo

Creek.[78] More importantly, Peters played a critical role in moving the permit application through the Forest Service bureaucracy.

Given his limited start-up funds, Healy had to be very careful about controlling costs during the initial development phase. One of the major shareholders, Oscar Murray, owned a local construction company and offered his equipment and labor to build the base area in exchange for his block of shares. The county government agreed to allocate funding to grade a five-thousand-foot access road linking the base area to the main road coming up from Bend. Meanwhile, Don Peters worked with the State Highway Commission on a plan that eventually added Century Drive to the state road system, allowing for snow removal by the Department of Transportation.[79]

Gene Gillis and Don Peters worked closely with Healy to select the site for the first runs and placement of the tow ropes. Gillis encouraged Healy to consider a new, European-made, 2,900-foot Poma lift, one of the first to be installed in the United States. The lift included two main towers at the beginning and end of the line, with six intermediate towers, and it was able to move over five hundred skiers per hour. However, that purchase and the installation expended around half of the corporation's initial shareholder funding.

Part of the plan included construction of a small day lodge close to the base of the Poma lift. The Forest Service assisted with the project's design, which included a ski shop, a first aid room, restrooms, a snack bar and a lounge with a fireplace.[80] Oscar Murray's construction company built the day lodge at a cost of around $35,000. With most of the funds allocated for infrastructure, Healy managed the initial development without taking a salary.

With opening set for the winter of 1958, there was still much work to be done during the final six months. Construction of the lodge and parking spaces for two hundred cars progressed into the fall while the Poma lift was still being assembled. Since water was unavailable at the base area, pit toilets were used for the first season, and potable water was delivered by truck from Bend.

Bachelor Butte opened for a trial run in mid-November 1958, with the first days of operation reserved for Skyliners members. In early December, a stretch of warm weather forced a brief closure of the ski area before it reopened over the holidays. However, due to a lack of funding, the hill operated only during weekends and holidays for its first season. The first days of normal operations attracted over eight hundred skiers. An all-day ticket for the Poma lift was $3.00 and it cost $1.50 to use the tow ropes.

Egan Lodge, circa 1959. *Deschutes County Historical Society.*

The day lodge was dedicated in January 1959 and named in honor of Deschutes National Forest supervisor James Egan. In his role as forest supervisor, Egan played a critical part in bringing the ski area to fruition; however, he didn't live to see it open after he died from leukemia in early 1958.[81]

During its first season, the area recorded around twenty-nine thousand skier visits.[82] Even during the first years of operation, around half of the resort's skiers came from outside Central Oregon, including most of the season ticket holders.[83] Importantly for the investors, the resort turned a small profit in its first year, which Healy convinced shareholders should be reinvested in the resort. Those funds enabled Healy to replace one of the two tow ropes with a T-bar lift and to complete some necessary upgrades to the pit toilets.

That early success continued into the second season, with thirty-six thousand skier visits during eighty-six days of operation. However, the facilities were already coming close to capacity, and there was a significant lack of parking. Nevertheless, the resort made another respectable profit in

BACHELOR BUTTE, CORP. 1958-59 RATES	November 7, 1958
Daily (all facilities including Rope Tows & Poma Lift)	$ 3.00
After 2:00 p.m.	$ 2.00
Single Ride Poma Lift	$ .50
Daily Rope Tows	$ 1.50
After 2:00 p.m.	$ 1.25
Season Tickets	
Family All Season	$85.00
Individual All Season	$50.00

Mt. Bachelor Ski Area

Above: Forest Service rangers supervising skiers on the rope tow, February 1958. *Deschutes National Forest.*

Left, top: Mt. Bachelor ski area ticket prices, 1958–59. *Courtesy of Steve Stenkamp.*

Left, bottom: Postcard showing the Poma lift with the main parking lot and Egan Lodge in the background, circa 1960. *Courtesy of Steve Stenkamp.*

its second year.[84] The Bend Chamber of Commerce estimated that skiers were already bringing around half a million dollars a year into the local economy. Hard work and support from the community had delivered on Healy's vision, placing Mt. Bachelor in a strong position as it entered the 1960s.

CHAPTER 3

MOUNT BACHELOR'S GROWTH YEARS

The 1960s was a period of rapid expansion for the ski industry, with annual growth rates of around 20 percent. Mt. Bachelor entered the new decade on financially solid ground and in a good position for continued expansion. The next phase included several critical decisions that would define the resort for generations. These included a commitment to maintaining local ownership and control over development and aggressively reinvesting profits into expansion and infrastructure improvements.

Much of the resort's early capital investment focused on expanding lift capacity and opening new terrain. Healy and other board members understood that this was critical for attracting skiers from outside Central Oregon and would enable the resort to grow. By the early 1960s, Mt. Bachelor was drawing over thirty-five thousand skier visits per year, which was already straining its infrastructure capacity. The parking lot often overflowed on weekends, and guests complained of long lines at the lifts.[85]

The first significant upgrade of the new decade was the installation of Mt. Bachelor's first double chairlift. After much research, Healy recommended a model from the Riblet Tramway Company of Spokane, Washington, that was already in use at several large resorts. At the time, Riblet was one of the largest ski chairlift manufacturers in the world. The company started out manufacturing mining tramways, but as that industry declined and skiing gained popularity, the company began designing lifts in the 1930s.

Riblet's first chairlift was installed in 1939 at Timberline on Mount Hood. Dubbed the Magic Mile, the lift reached one thousand vertical feet and

A line of skiers waiting for the Poma lift, with the ski-tracked Egan Cone in the background, circa 1960. *Photograph by Ray Atkeson. Copyright Ray Atkeson Image Archive.*

extended a mile above the iconic lodge. When installed, it was the longest chairlift in the world. Riblet eventually built more than four hundred lifts, primarily in Washington, Oregon and California, and once had the largest number of double chairlifts operating in the United States.[86]

Mt. Bachelor's new Riblet double chairlift cost around $130,000 to purchase and install, more than the entire start-up investment for the ski area in 1958. To finance the equipment, the board approved the issue of additional shares of common stock and took out a mortgage loan.[87] The chairlift was installed over the summer of 1961 and opened that November.

The new lift was known initially as the Chair, later called Chair One and finally renamed Black Chair. It was located on the Coffee run to the east of the Egan Lodge. The lift was 4,420 feet in length, rising to approximately 7,700 feet with an endpoint slightly lower and to the east of today's Pine Marten lift.[88] It had ninety seats with a capacity of 680 skiers per hour and a transit time of nine minutes from the bottom to the top.

HIRING NEW STAFF

Other important decisions made during those early years involved selecting key staff members who would shape the resort as it matured into a regional destination. One of those individuals was Cliff Blann, hired as the mountain manager after the first manager, "Jop" Morgan, retired in 1961. Blann helped maintain the machinery during the first season and installed much of the original equipment. He also oversaw road and hill operations.

Blann was an exceptional athlete and skier; in 1937–38, he won the Underdahl trophy, which was awarded to Oregon's outstanding junior skier. Blann was a member of the Skyliners' rescue unit when it became part of the National Ski Patrol System in 1938.[89] He later served in World War II with the Eighty-Second Airborne Division in the South Pacific. Blann had climbed and skied Bachelor Butte many times before the resort's opening and came into the job with an intimate knowledge of the terrain. He served as mountain manager for the next twenty-four years, leaving an indelible mark on the staff, the guests and the community.

Mt. Bachelor initially operated the ski school as a concession, and Healy hired Joe Ward to run the operation. Ward had been an instructor in Sun Valley, Idaho, before moving to Bend in 1957. He ran the school for several

Cliff Blann driving one of Mt. Bachelor's Thiokol Spryte snowcats, circa 1966. *Photograph by Don Peters, Deschutes National Forest.*

Jack Meissner at Willamette Pass on his winter ski tour of the Skyline Trail, 1948. *Photograph courtesy of Jane Meissner.*

years with the help of his wife, Wanda. During that time, Jack and Virginia Meissner began driving to Bend on weekends from their home on Odell Lake to teach at the ski school. Jack was already a well-known figure in Oregon's ski community from his job at Willamette Pass.

In 1948, Jack Meissner set out on an epic three-hundred-mile ski tour from Mount Hood to Crater Lake. In mid-February, he left Timberline Lodge with forty-five pounds of gear, heading out along the Skyline Trail. Due to heavy snow and difficult travel, his partner soon dropped out of the trip. Meissner continued alone, relying on prearranged supply drops by the Civil Air Patrol. After a grueling thirty-three days of travel, ranging in elevation from four to ten thousand feet, Meissner arrived at Crater Lake Lodge in early April, becoming the first person to accomplish such a journey during winter.[90]

Jack and Virginia eventually moved to Bend in the early 1960s. They took over the ski school concession and ran it until July 1973, when management decided to end the concession and bring the ski school inside the corporation.[91] Jack went on to run ski schools at Bogus Basin in Idaho and Willamette Pass. Virginia remained in Bend and became a

Virginia Meissner preparing for a race at Willamette Pass, circa 1944. *Photograph courtesy of Jane Meissner.*

central figure in the development of Central Oregon's cross-country skiing community and a driving force in creating the Meissner Sno-Park along Cascade Lakes Highway.

David Marsh was another consequential hire of the early years. After moving to Bend from the Oregon coast, Marsh began his career at Mt. Bachelor, working part-time as a rope tow operator in the late 1960s and eventually becoming part of the ski patrol. Marsh earned the trust of Blann and Healy and gradually worked his way up, becoming the operations manager in 1979, vice president of operations in 1984 and executive vice president the following year. In 1988, he was named president and CEO, a position he held for ten years.[92]

During his long tenure, Marsh worked closely with Healy and was involved in nearly all the significant developments at Mt. Bachelor, including installing numerous chairlifts and constructing the Pine Marten Lodge. Marsh was also closely involved in creating the Mt. Bachelor Ski Education Foundation and other programs.

CONTINUING INFRASTRUCTURE IMPROVEMENTS

Beyond the new state-of-the-art Riblet chairlift, the resort lacked many essential services and amenities around the base area. After several years of operation, it was still using pit toilets and didn't have on-site potable water. The lifts and base operations relied on a diesel engine for electricity, and there was insufficient lodge space for guests. Healy was aware that the ski area needed significant investment to move forward; however, he was also determined to keep the business under local ownership and control.[93] This meant finding a way to raise funds among existing shareholders or through loans.

Healy applied for a Small Business Administration line of credit while the board approved the sale of additional stock shares to finance the next development phase. With funding secured, Healy embarked on several important projects, including expansion of the Egan Lodge, adding extra parking spaces and installing a second Riblet double chairlift. The new chairlift, adjacent to Egan Cone and later named Red Chair, was complete in 1965.[94]

The decision to continue pushing profits back into expansion brought a steady increase in skier numbers. The 1964–65 season saw over one hundred thousand lift tickets sold and more the following year. Two new lifts were planned during the late 1960s to deal with long wait times, and a third Riblet double chair, later called Yellow Chair, was added in 1967. The base was located east of Chair Two (Red Chair), replacing the original T-bar.

Another important initiative was an effort to develop overnight lodging at the base area. Initially, Healy had to convince a skeptical business community of the need for such accommodations, explaining that they were necessary for Mt. Bachelor to compete with other resorts.[95] After gaining support from the Chamber of Commerce, the board approved a five-year contract to build and operate the lodge with a group of five shareholders. Felix Marcoulier was named general manager and assumed responsibility for operations and services.[96]

The opening was delayed until the 1966 season, but eventually, the lodge was complete, featuring sixteen single-room suites and eight two-room suites with kitchens and private baths. The lodge had a full kitchen with a chef serving evening meals for overnight guests and offered vacation packages that included lift tickets, food and ski lessons.[97] The same year the lodge opened, Mt. Bachelor set another attendance record, with over 110,000 visitors that season.[98]

Mt. Bachelor's overnight lodge, circa 1966. *Deschutes County Historical Society.*

The overnight lodge was eventually sold to Mount Bachelor Inc. in early 1968 and Vince Genna, the recreation director for Bend, was hired as the new general manager. However, operating overnight accommodations created numerous management challenges that eventually led to a critical decision by the board to close the facility in 1971. When Healy announced the decision, he explained, "We've learned that we do not want to be hotel keepers. That is a field that rightfully belongs to facilities in Bend and other nearby areas."[99] After only five years of operation, the building closed for renovation and eventually repurposed as the new West Village Lodge.

At the same time, Mt. Bachelor announced a quarter of a million dollars in new infrastructure investments, including adding a fourth chairlift, later known as Blue Chair, in time for the 1970–71 season. The fourth chairlift increased the resort's overall lift capacity to over 4,100 skiers per hour. Other upgrades that year included the addition of a new "mini lodge" with a warming area, restrooms and first-aid facilities and two hundred additional parking spaces off the access road.[100]

The decision to close the lodge and forego development of on-site accommodations was significant for several reasons. As Mt. Bachelor grew,

Healy preferred to partner with local hotels and businesses rather than compete against them. This decision reflected Healy's original outlook, viewing Mt. Bachelor as a civic project for the good of the community rather than a strictly moneymaking venture. However, as the ski industry evolved, that decision would also limit Mt. Bachelor's growth, as other resorts aggressively pursued slope-side development and amenities to attract new customers.

As Mt. Bachelor ended its first decade, Healy and the board were aware of industry trends and the challenge of attracting skiers from beyond Central Oregon. Although some people considered Mt. Bachelor a "locals" spot, by the early 1960s, well over half of all season passes were being purchased by skiers from other parts of Oregon and surrounding states. By the mid-1970s, an informal survey suggested that only around of one-quarter of the skiers using the mountain were from Central Oregon.

As the resort entered its second decade, Mt. Bachelor was already having a noticeable impact on the local economy, confirming the prophecy of Nils Wulfsberg dating back to the 1920s that the region could become a mecca for winter sports. Alana Audette, a former president and CEO of the Central Oregon Visitors Association, credits Bill Healy with planting the seed of that transformation, describing him as "one of the single strongest influences for the transition from a lumber to a tourism-based community."[101]

As the resort's profile grew, Mount Bachelor even earned a cameo role in a 1967 big-budget Hollywood western starring Kirk Douglas, Robert Mitchum and Sally Field in her motion picture debut. The movie, *The Way West*, was filmed at several locations around Central Oregon, including Smith Rock, Sunriver and along the Deschutes River. The movie's climactic scene, depicting a wagon train struggling over the Oregon Trail, was shot on Mount Bachelor's slopes with Broken Top in the background. One reviewer from the *Oregonian* hinted that the film might have been "the worst western ever made."[102]

With its growing popularity, the resort was becoming a catalyst for other investors looking to build the region's tourism-based economy. One prominent example was the development of Sunriver, first conceived in the late 1950s as Mt. Bachelor began operations. The resort was established on the former grounds of Camp Abbot, an Army Corps of Engineers training center during World War II. The camp was named for General Henry Larcom Abbot, a West Point graduate and military engineer who led a railroad survey party through the area in 1855.[103] Camp Abbot opened in December 1942, with the first trainees arriving in March 1943.

Left: Climactic scene on the slopes of Bachelor Butte from *The Way West*, 1967. *United Artists.*

Below: Camp Abbot main gate with Bachelor Butte visible in the background, circa 1943. *Deschutes County Historical Society*

16-405 Main Entrance – Camp Abbott

During the camp's first year of operation, more than ninety thousand combat engineers were trained at the site. The camp operated until the summer of 1944. After the war, most of the facilities were demolished, except for the officer's club, now known as the resort's Great Hall. After the war, the Prineville-based Hudspeth Land and Livestock Company purchased the land from the government.[104] The land initially reverted to cattle grazing; however, its value for recreation and development was evident. With improvements to the Dalles–California Highway in the mid-

1950s, the area had better access for visitors arriving from the Willamette Valley and California.

In 1958, the Hudspeth family formed Recreation Unlimited, hoping to turn the area into a fee-based recreation site. However, due to financial difficulties, the property was sold to Portland lawyer Don McCallum and developer John Gray. The two men consolidated over one hundred individual parcels of land and began working on Sunriver's original master plan in 1965. By 1968, Sunriver Properties Inc. was established with McCallum as president. Construction began the same year.[105]

Like Bill Healy, the developers of Sunriver understood that the resort would not succeed unless it attracted visitors from outside Central Oregon. The master plan called for a planned community of twelve to fifteen thousand residents, hoping to draw second-home owners and retirees from around Oregon and West Coast metropolitan areas. The design concept emphasized preserving the area's natural beauty with strict controls on development. The location offered easy access to nature trails, recreation and nearby skiing on Mount Bachelor.

Until 1983, Sunriver residents had to drive thirty-eight miles through Bend to reach Mount Bachelor. There was also an alternate twenty-eight-mile "shortcut" using an old Brooks-Scanlon logging road between Sunriver and the Inn of the Seventh Mountain that was drivable, weather permitting. However, when the Forest Service stopped maintaining that road, Sunriver Properties paid $800,000 to fully pave and maintain the road between Sunriver and Century Drive along the present route of NF-45 (Edison Ice Cave Road). The road opened just before the 1983 ski season. Bill Healy presided over the ribbon-cutting ceremony and rode in the first car to cover the seventeen miles of new highway between Sunriver and the ski resort.[106]

PLANNING FOR THE FUTURE

Through the 1960s, much of Mt. Bachelor's growth was based on incremental investments as funding became available. The board's decision to stick with local investors ultimately limited its access to capital. However, it also kept decision-making close to home and ensured that management was responsive to community interests. Yet, as skier numbers continued to rise, Healy and the board realized that they needed outside expertise to develop a long-range strategy for the future.

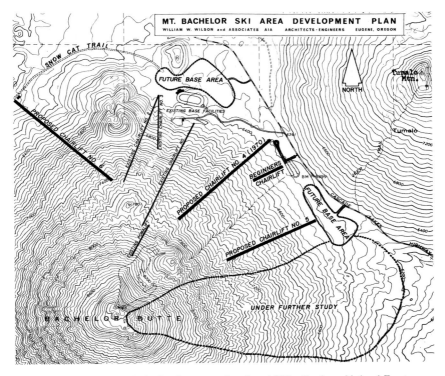

Schematic of Mt. Bachelor's development plan, late 1960s. *Deschutes National Forest.*

Healy brought in Nelson Bennet, an old friend from his World War II service in Italy with the Tenth Mountain Division. Bennet had raced on the ski team at the University of New Hampshire before the war and later worked in Sun Valley. After the war, he returned to the ski industry and later served as team manager of the U.S. Olympic Alpine Team at the 1956 winter games in Cortina d'Ampezzo, Italy. Bennet eventually became the general manager at the White Pass Ski Area in Washington and a ski area development consultant.[107]

After reviewing operations at Mt. Bachelor, Bennet offered a long list of suggested improvements, including rerouting access roads, adding parking, installing new chairlifts and upgrading the base facilities. With these considerations in mind, the board submitted a proposed twenty-year plan for Forest Service approval.[108] The Forest Service approved the concept in 1972 and granted the resort a thirty-year permit. Before then, Mt. Bachelor had operated under a yearly special-use permit that made long-range planning difficult.

With a new strategy in place and the Forest Service's blessing, the next step involved securing financing to move forward with the plan. The previous decade had seen a 92 percent growth in ticket sales, averaging around 150,000 annual skier visits.[109] Based on the resort's solid financial record and growth rate, Healy could secure a loan if he found guarantors who would back the loan amount. This meant bringing on additional investors and expanding the company's board of directors.

Among the new investors was Dean Papé of Eugene, an Oregon State graduate and founder of the Papé Group, a heavy equipment dealer started in 1938. Another new investor was Wallace Stevenson, head of a family lumber business in White Salmon, Washington. Stevenson had won the Bronze Star medal in 1944 during D-Day while commanding a submarine chaser. Both Papé and Stevenson were friends of Healy.

Brooks Resources, by then a subsidiary of the Brooks-Scanlon Company, also provided backing for the loan. At that time, the company was working on its first resort development project at Black Butte Ranch and starting a new condominium project along Century Drive, later known as Mount Bachelor Village.

The new round of funding enabled Mt. Bachelor to move forward on two new lifts. By then, the lift-naming convention had changed from numbers to

The Monster on the summit of Bachelor Butte. Built by Tucker Sno-Cat of Grants Pass, Oregon. *Courtesy of Tucker Sno-Cat.*

colors. The new Green Chair (originally named Button) was another Riblet double, roughly following the path of the current Skyliner Express. Next was the Orange Chair (originally called Murray Meadow), with its base near the West Village Lodge. That chair was the first Riblet triple to be installed in Oregon and had the capacity to move 1,800 skiers per hour.[110] The Orange and Green Chairs were constructed during the summer of 1973 and went into operation for the 1973–74 season.

The mid-1970s saw a significant expansion of skier terrain with the opening of a new lift on the mountain's northwestern side. The Outback Chair was a Riblet double and cost $2 million to install, opening in the winter of 1976. Before then, skiers accessed the westside area using a Sno-Cat, dubbed "the monster," that Healy had purchased from Tucker Sno-Cat Corporation of Medford, Oregon. The vehicle was among a handful of specialized Tucker 800s that the company built for service in Antarctica.[111]

Tucker Sno-Cat was founded by Emmitt Tucker of Grants Pass, Oregon. The company began building snow machines in the 1930s, and its vehicles were eventually used at many resorts for trail grooming, snow removal, search and rescue and avalanche control. The year Mt. Bachelor opened, the English explorer Sir Vivian Fuchs used four Tuckers 800s to complete the first overland crossing of Antarctica.[112]

After the Outback Chair opened, the Tucker Sno-Cat was used for maintenance work and transporting skiers to the top of Mount Bachelor until the summit lift opened in 1983. Today, the family-owned Tucker Corporation, based in Medford, Oregon, is considered the oldest manufacturer of snow machines in the world.

ESTABLISHING MT. BACHELOR'S NORDIC CENTER

During the late 1960s, cross-country skiing was gaining popularity as a few resorts began offering groomed trails, lessons and basic amenities for the sport. By the early 1970s, Mt. Bachelor had only a few kilometers of snowmobile-groomed trails running between the Black and Green Chairs around the present area of the Skyliner lift.[113] The ski school director, Jack Meissner, groomed the trails using his own Ski-Doo Alpine snowmobile, dragging along a track-setter. Meanwhile, Virginia Meissner taught cross-country lessons from the alpine ski school, taking students out on ungroomed trails around what is now the West Village parking lot.[114]

Bob Mathews first proposed a formal cross-country network to Bill Healy in March 1976 in a one-page memo with a plan for new trails and grooming. Mathews had relocated to Bend from Minnesota in 1973 and was working at the ski school. With Healy's blessing, he developed two new loops for the 1976–77 season. The original Loop A was a two-kilometer trail along the Cascade Lakes Highway. Loop B was a five-kilometer trail tracing the edge of Dutchman Flat outside Mt. Bachelor's special-use permit area.

When the first two trails were established, Mt. Bachelor had the only regularly groomed Nordic system among Oregon's alpine ski areas.[115] The following season, Mathews added a five-kilometer training loop circling the Old Maid butte with the help of former Olympic biathlete Jay Bowerman, who had used the route for his training during the early 1970s.[116]

During the first few seasons, profits from overall mountain operations helped subsidize the cross-country center. Mathews did most of the grooming using the resort's first snowmobile, a Rupp American model made in Mansfield, Ohio. The Nordic Center had around two thousand skier visits during the first season, but that number increased steadily. With its early success, Healy continued supporting the expansion of the program.[117] The cross-country center eventually moved into a four-hundred-square-foot trailer in the parking area. Mathews shared a Tucker Sno-Cat with the mountain manager, Cliff Blann, for daily grooming.[118] Later, the Nordic department received its own Tucker Sno-Cat, which it used for several seasons.

By the early 1980s, the Nordic Center had around twenty kilometers of groomed trails covering a footprint similar to today's network. The additional trails included Beginner's Luck, Jay's, Woody's Way, Easy Back and First Time. The Zig Zag trail was added for the 1982–83 season, extending the network to twenty-five kilometers. Devecka's was added the following year, increasing the network to thirty-two kilometers.[119] As the center expanded, so did skier numbers. By 1979, Nordic skier visits increased to around seven thousand annually.[120] By the 1983–84 season, that number had nearly doubled to over twelve thousand skier visits per year.[121]

During his early years as Nordic sports director, Mathews was assisted by another recent transplant to Bend named Bob Woodward. The two men ran ski camps and races, including the Cascade Crest Ski Marathon, which ran from Bachelor Butte to Little Lava Lake and back, beginning in 1979. While working as a freelance sportswriter, Woodward wrote numerous articles in national publications putting Mt. Bachelor's Nordic Center on the map and attracting top-ranked skiers for training and competition.[122]

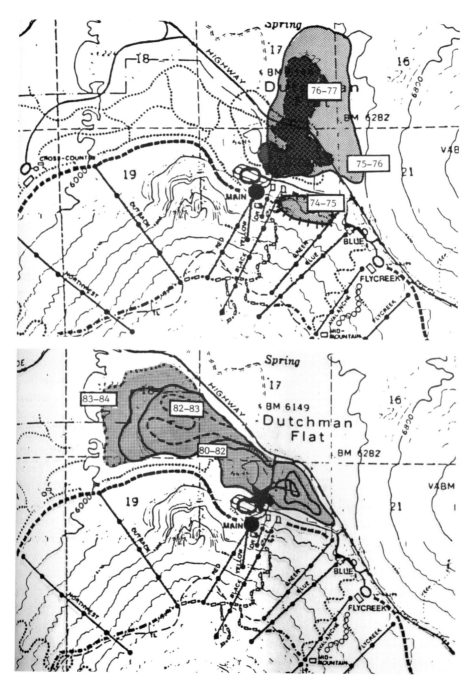

Expansion of the Nordic network, 1974–84. *Courtesy of Diane Armpriest.*

Nordic Skiing

$2.00
OCTOBER 1980

Gore-Tex Boots
Inside Story On
Outer Layer Fiber

Ski Poles
What To Buy and
How To Use Them

Aerobic Fitness
Training Procedures
and Exercise Formula

Sierra Nevadas
Skiing Where Mountain Passes Lie Above The Clouds

The first Nordic Center director, Bob Mathews, circa 1980. *Photograph by Bob Woodward.*

In addition to his work at the Nordic Center, Woodward became a local mountain-biking legend and founder of the Central Oregon Trail Alliance. From 1997 to 1999, Woodard served as the mayor of Bend and was once dubbed "America's only mountain-biking mayor."[123] In 2012, Woodward was inducted into the Mountain Bike Hall of Fame. Woody's Way, a popular loop trail on the Nordic network, is named in his honor.

Another member of the early Nordic staff was Dennis Oliphant, a former ski racer from the University of Oregon. Oliphant arrived in Bend in 1977 and worked various jobs at the center, from instruction to grooming.[124] He was instrumental in developing the junior cross-country racing program and coached for many years. Oliphant later served as the first Nordic program director for the Mt. Bachelor Sports Education Foundation and was a longtime board member. He was the founder and CEO of Sun Country Tours, which he started in 1978 and later sold to Powdr Enterprises in 2016.

As the Nordic Center grew, it gained a reputation as a premier training site for elite-level competitors. In the late 1970s, Mt. Bachelor began hosting the annual Fischer-Swix-Salomon cross-country ski camps, run by Woodward. Around the same time, the U.S. National Nordic team held its first spring training camp at the center in preparation for the 1984 Winter Olympics in Sarajevo. To entice the national squad to Mt. Bachelor, Healy promised free grooming for the duration of the training camp. In the early 1980s, the center hosted several major race events, including the FIS Cross-Country Nor-Am Cup in 1984, a high-level competition just below the World Cup level. In 1985, the Nordic Center was chosen as the site for the U.S. cross-country national championship.

By the early 1980s, the Nordic program had outgrown its cramped parking-lot trailers and moved into a dedicated lodge on the northern edge of the West Village parking area. A new log-cabin-style lodge was designed by local architect Vernon Sexton, who also helped develop the Pine Marten and Sunrise Lodges and the summit chairlift.

The 3,800-square-foot lodge opened in November 1983 and included a rental department, a cafe, a retail area and a space for instructors and ski patrol. By that time, the network was around thirty-five kilometers of groomed trails, with the addition of a new trail along the old catchline on the mountain's northwest aspect. The following year, the center received its first dedicated grooming machine, a Pistenbully 170.

By the late 1980s, the Nordic Center's reputation was firmly established within the cross-county community. In 1989, Mt. Bachelor hosted the annual convention of the Cross Country Ski Areas Association (CCSAA), drawing

BACHELOR'S NEW LODGE FOR NORDIC SKIERS

Artist's rendition of the new Nordic Center Lodge, circa 1983. *Sketch by Gary Johansen.*

industry leaders from around the country. By that time, the network was close to its present configuration. The last few trails were added in the late 1980s and early 1990s, including Oli's Alley, Leslie's Lunge, Rich's Range and Easy Up.

When Bob Mathews departed as the Nordic director in 1991, the network was nearly fifty-six kilometers and attracting around thirty thousand skier visits per year. Mathews credits much of the center's early success to Bill Healy's support of cross-country skiing when the sport was still a niche winter pastime, generating only a small portion of the mountain's overall revenue.

Today, Mt. Bachelor has Oregon's most extensive cross-country trail systems and one of the longest seasons of any resort in North America, often extending through the end of May. It remains a frequent site for the spring training camps of the U.S. and Canadian National Nordic Teams and the U.S. Biathlon and Paralympic Teams.

CENTRAL OREGON'S CROSS-COUNTRY SKIING ROYALTY: VIRGINIA MEISSNER

Virginia (Tompkins) Meissner was a pioneer of cross-country skiing in Central Oregon. Born in Salem in 1925, Virginia joined the outdoor club while a student at the University of Oregon and became a frequent skier at Willamette Pass. She led an active outdoor life as a member of the Obsidians and competed in alpine and cross-country ski races. Virginia later worked as a ski instructor at Willamette Pass, where she met her husband, Jack Meissner.[125]

Jack and Virginia moved to Bend in the early 1960s and took over the ski school concession at Bachelor Butte. Virginia later taught outdoor education at Central Oregon Community College and was an active member of the Professional Ski Instructors of America.[126] Along with Jack, she helped write the original cross-country teaching manual for the Pacific Northwest Ski Instructors Association (PNSIA) and established instructor certification standards. Over the years, the Meissners trained dozens of future instructors.

Virginia authored several popular guidebooks, including *Cross Country Ski Tours in Central Oregon*, and was among the founders of the Central Oregon Nordic Club, serving as its president in 1987. During the 1970s, she

Virginia Meissner leading a ski tour on Wikiup Plain near South Sister. *Courtesy of Jane Meissner.*

petitioned the Forest Service to designate the area around Swampy Lakes for nonmotorized recreation and Sno-Parks along the Cascade Lakes Highway. In 1989, the Forest Service posthumously named the Tangent ski area in her honor. Today, the Virginia Meissner Sno-Park is one of the most popular winter recreation sites in Central Oregon, providing access to forty-seven kilometers of community-supported cross-country ski and snowshoe trails.

SUMMIT FEVER

As the 1970s ended, Bill Healy set his sights on another ambitious project: building a lift to the summit of Bachelor Butte. The proposed chairlift would enable skiers to access the entire mountain, with breathtaking views and three thousand vertical feet of skiing. The plan would require several million dollars to construct the lift while potentially altering the mountain's landscape permanently.

Healy's vision for reaching the summit became a driving goal entering the new decade. However, as he was looking ahead, the previous decade underscored the precariousness of the resort's success thus far. Two crises during the era demonstrated that many factors determining success or failure were beyond Healy's control—specifically, the economy and the weather.

The oil shock of the early 1970s became a crisis for the resort and the entire region. Worries over gas availability led local boosters to build a parking lot along Century Drive, encouraging skiers to carpool. Area merchants sponsored a free shuttle bus from the airport in Redmond and offered special discounts for weekend hotels, hoping that guests would not cancel vacations as gas prices skyrocketed.[127] By that time, tourism and recreation supported thousands of jobs in Central Oregon. The industry downturn had a significant ripple effect on the local economy, particularly for the developers of vacation properties.

The oil crisis and recession of 1973–74 coincided with the initial phase of development for Sunriver Resort. Lagging unit sales forced the developers to transfer around 2,200 acres of the property to the Deschutes National Forest to cover losses. However, the market gradually improved through the 1970s, putting development back on track.

Newly established Brooks Resources faced similar challenges as it began a large development project along Century Drive, the Ski House condominiums, later renamed Mount Bachelor Village. Before the oil shock, during the project's initial phase, Brooks had presold every unit.

However, the recession led the company to release investors from their purchase agreements. Every buyer took the offer, except for Bill Healy, who kept his contract.[128]

Another unpredictable challenge came from the weather. Bachelor Butte is blessed with an abundant and reliable snowpack; however, snowfall for the 1976–77 season was far below average. After the previous record-breaking season, that winter proved a disaster, leading to significant losses for the resort and the local businesses dependent on ski-related tourism. There was no snow in November that year and not enough in December for the resort to open before the holidays. While January brought some relief, a warm spell and rain in February forced Healy to furlough his staff. Conditions improved slightly by springtime but not enough to salvage the season.

Nevertheless, the decade ended with Mt. Bachelor on solid footing. The 1978–79 season was a good year financially, and early snow in 1979 permitted the lifts to open during the first week in November. At the time, the board was preparing an ambitious master plan for Forest Service review. The project involved a new lodge building, upgrades to power and water supplies, additional parking, new equipment for grooming, and installing up to ten new lifts, including the proposed summit lift.[129] As proposed, the plan involved an unprecedented investment aiming to put Mt. Bachelor on the map as a world-class destination.

CHAPTER 4

TO THE SUMMIT

D espite the oil shock, a recession and disastrous weather during the 1976–77 season, Mt. Bachelor remained profitable through a challenging period. The 1970s saw steady growth in revenue and earnings, with continued increases in skier visits. Several major infrastructure projects offered an improved guest experience, including opening new terrain with the addition of the Outback Chair, renovation of the day lodge and expansion of the Nordic network. Meanwhile, other important projects were on the horizon as the resort neared its twenty-fifth anniversary.

In the spring of 1979, Bachelor Inc. reached an agreement with the Forest Service on a conceptual master plan for future development. The board hired the firm Diethelm and Bressler of Eugene to assemble a detailed study guiding the proposal.[130] Based on that study, Mt. Bachelor presented a revised master plan to the Forest Service in early 1980.

That plan envisioned an ambitious program for continued growth, which projected an increase of daily visitors from around 7,000 skiers per day to over 21,000.[131] Those figures assumed that Mt. Bachelor would attract over 1 million annual skier visits within ten to fifteen years—double the record-setting 1979–80 season, when about 480,000 skiers visited the mountain. This would require increasing transportation and parking capacity from two thousand vehicles per day to over five thousand.[132]

The proposal included two new day lodges in the Flycreek area and at mid-mountain (eventually the Sunrise and Pine Marten Lodges). It called for eight new lifts and expansion of the Nordic facilities near the West Village

Bill Healy discussing the resort's 1980 master development plan during a meeting with the Forest Service. Undated photo. *Deschutes National Forest.*

base area. The plan also included communications upgrades and improved water access and power systems. The existing water supply, drawn from a tributary of Todd Creek, had been in use since 1964 and was no longer adequate for the resort's needs.[133]

Of all the proposals outlined in the new master plan, perhaps the one most reflective of Bill Healy's vision was the summit lift. Healy had been focused on this goal for years and had conducted preliminary feasibility studies on the summit's topography, avalanche risk, winds and snow conditions. In addition to being challenging from an engineering standpoint, the proposed summit lift would dramatically transform the resort's character.[134]

Healy understood that adding new terrain and increasing the resort's vertical drop to around three thousand feet would put it on the map as a major ski destination. The proposal noted that "Mount Bachelor could become the most popular destination resort area in the West," giving Bend "the potential to become a year-round tourist resort comparable to Lake Placid or Squaw Valley."[135]

Some shareholders were skeptical about the enormous investments required to realize the ambitious goals outlined in the master plan. However, others recognized the potential impact of such an expansion on the local economy. According to data compiled as part of the proposal, the resort already generated around 20 percent of the region's overall tourism dollars and 80 percent of winter business for local hotels and resorts.[136]

Based on a multiplier analysis, Mt. Bachelor was generating approximately $25 million in direct income for local hotels, restaurants and businesses and $67 million in total revenue. Skier-related services accounted for over 3,000 local jobs, or around 16 percent of the labor force. Visitor data also showed that most visitors skiing at Mt. Bachelor were coming from outside Central Oregon, providing an essential boost for the local economy during the winter season. Mt. Bachelor's planning figures estimated that the proposed expansion would bring in an additional $18–20 million to the economy while adding 210 more seasonal jobs on the mountain.[137]

After receiving the master plan, the Forest Service conducted its environmental assessment and identified several areas of concern in the proposal. The most significant decision involved constructing a service road to the summit for installing the lift apparatus. Forest supervisor David Mohla initially approved the summit lift plan but without construction of the service road, citing public concerns over the road's visual impact on the landscape.[138]

Healy was discouraged by the decision but not defeated. He told the local paper that "the summit chair will be built, road or no road."[139] The Oregon Wilderness Coalition director, Jim Monteith, was among the plan's fiercest opponents. The protest against the summit lift was aided by members of the Sierra Club and the Wilderness Society, a grassroots organization started in 1974 with the goal of protecting roadless areas across Oregon.[140]

Pressure from Monteith and the Oregon Wilderness Coalition was the first significant instance of environmentalist pushback against development plans for Mount Bachelor. The ensuing decades would see the ski industry involved in many similar disputes as it opened new areas for development. While attempting to adjudicate a path forward among competing interests, the Forest Service often became stuck in the middle.

In the case of the summit lift, Healy met with Monteith to discuss the proposal and reportedly felt that the two sides could reach a compromise. Healy eventually filed a protest with the Forest Service, arguing that the service road would not detrimentally impact the view of Mount Bachelor from Bend and the road to Sunriver. The Forest Service ultimately reversed its decision and allowed for the construction of the service road.

Monteith was reportedly furious when he heard about the change. He accused the Forest Service of ignoring environmental considerations and

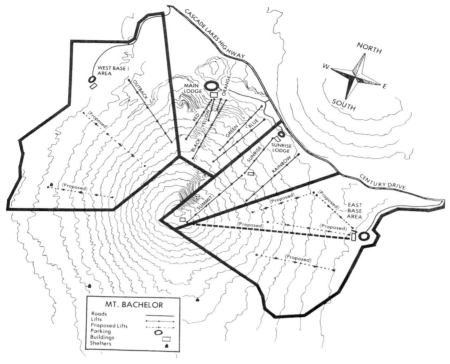

Schematic of Mt. Bachelor's development plan, circa 1980s. *Deschutes National Forest.*

placing corporate priorities over conservation.[141] However, as the design plans progressed, the engineers eventually opted for a strategy that didn't require a service road. Despite their earlier disagreement, Healy called Monteith to tell him that the road would not be built.

While the summit lift may have been the most ambitious aspect of the master plan, the plan contained several other proposals that would transform the face of the resort. It called for developing a new base-area complex that would open new terrain on Mount Bachelor's east side. Expansion into this area and construction of the Flycreek Chair (later renamed Rainbow Chair) was a critical element linked to development of the summit lift.

The Rainbow Chair, completed in 1980, was Mt. Bachelor's first Yan lift, built by Lift Engineering of Carson City, Nevada. The following year, the Sunrise Chair, another Yan triple, was completed in front of Flycreek Lodge, later renamed Sunrise Lodge. Plans for the new lodge included a full-service base area with a restaurant and bar, rentals, a ski school, a first aid room and a retail area. The proposed east base facilities were designed to accommodate five thousand skiers with an additional 1,000–1,200 parking spots.

Development of the Sunrise base area reflected Healy's vision for moving the resort toward year-round operations. The master plan envisioned using the new Sunrise Lodge as a base for educational programs and recreational activities including hiking trails, sightseeing lift rides to the summit and an alpine slide.[142] Ultimately, the Forest Service didn't approve the alpine slide but supported other plans to expand the resort's offerings beyond winter recreation.

Notably, the master plan did not contain a proposal for overnight accommodations, except for RV parking. The Forest Service remained opposed to the development of overnight accommodations inside the permit area. Healy was satisfied with that decision, having no desire to turn Mt. Bachelor into a destination resort or to compete against local hotels, restaurants and vacation developments closer to town. Healy insisted that "when skiers think of Mount Bachelor, they think of downtown Bend."[143]

Bill Healy breaks ground on the Flycreek (later Sunrise) Lodge. Undated photo. *Deschutes National Forest.*

With the Forest Service's blessing, work began on the summit lift, with plans to open in time for Mt. Bachelor's twenty-fifth anniversary in 1983. Healy personally selected the Doppelmayr triple chair to reach the summit. Several years before, Doppelmayr had built the world's first detachable quad chair in Breckenridge, Colorado. The new technology significantly increased lift speed and capacity over the earlier-generation fixed-grip apparatus. The summit triple chair, originally called the Silver Streak Express, would move over 2,150 skiers per hour, with safer passenger loading and unloading.

Another critical feature of the Doppelmayr triple was its detachable chairs, which could be removed at night or during periods of severe weather. This was particularly important for Mt. Bachelor's summit operations, which frequently experienced high winds and storm conditions. The ability to pull the chairs during storm cycles reduced the accumulation of ice and snow, making it easier to reopen when conditions cleared.

Work on the summit lift began in late 1982 with the construction of temporary towers and the upper and lower terminal buildings. At nearly 5,000 feet long and climbing over 1,700 vertical feet, the lift required twenty-one towers to reach the top. The lift arrived from Europe in sections, and workers assembled the apparatus in the parking lot before moving the pieces up the mountain by truck and helicopter. By the fall of 1983, the project remained on schedule, with the grand opening planned for December.[144]

Healy remained closely involved throughout the project's duration, often flying over the mountain in a helicopter to inspect the work. However, his pace was slowing somewhat due to health concerns. After experiencing an unexplained weakness in 1981, Healy was diagnosed with amyotrophic lateral sclerosis, or Lou Gehrig's disease.[145]

While Healy remained focused on implementing the master plan and completion of the summit lift, he stopped skiing and scaled back his pace of work. His declining energy and mobility issues eventually required redistributing responsibility among the board's leadership. Dean Papé became cochairman of the board and assumed responsibility for business aspects, while David Marsh moved up to the vice president position.

Another major personnel transition involved the retirement of Cliff Blann, who had managed operations on the mountain since 1961. After twenty-four years, Blann knew the mountain better than anyone. He had overseen a dramatic transformation of the ski area, from two tow ropes and the original Poma lift to ten chairlifts with 360 degrees of skiable terrain off the summit.

Skiers riding Mt. Bachelor's new summit lift with Tumalo Mountain in the background, 1983. *Deschutes National Forest.*

Despite the economic recession of the early 1980s, Mt. Bachelor enjoyed steady increases in skier numbers and visitors from a broadening geographic range. By 1983, around 35 percent of Mt. Bachelor's skiers were from out of state. Roughly 16 percent came from Washington State and slightly more from California.[146] These out-of-state guests represented Mt. Bachelor's fastest-growing segment of business, spurred by new direct flights from Northern California and other large metropolitan markets.

The 1986–87 season was another banner year with a record 635,000 skier visits and plans for continuing expansion. The old Black double chair (originally Chair One) was replaced by the new Pine Marten Express chair, a Doppelmayr high-speed quad with a capacity of 2,800 skiers per hour. At the time, it was the fastest chair on the mountain.

The following year came the addition of the Outback Express, another Doppelmayr high-speed quad with a similar capacity. The new chair added several new runs on the mountain's northwest aspect, while the original Outback Chair, constructed in 1976, remained as a backup until 1990. The new Outback Chair was followed in 1989 by the Skyliner Express. The new Doppelmayr high-speed quad with detachable chairs increased the resort's overall lift capacity to nearly twenty thousand skiers per hour.

Other infrastructure projects included improvements to the West Village parking area, significant renovations and expansion of the main lodge and constructing a new guest services building and maintenance facilities. The final project topping off a decade of breakneck development was the construction of the Pine Marten Lodge at mid-mountain.

Bend architect Vernon Sexton, who had worked on several other buildings at Mt. Bachelor, designed the lodge. Sexton and the Bend-based Kirby Nagelhout Construction Company had a goal of completing the project quickly between the 1987 and 1988 seasons.[147] The original proposal called for a more traditional wooden-frame lodge; however, Sexton and Nagelhout opted for a concrete design with extra rebar for added strength due to harsh weather conditions at mid-mountain.

The construction team began manufacturing lodge components even before Sexton finalized the design. The crew started pouring the concrete foundation in May while snow remained on the ground. Workers and equipment had to navigate a two-mile dirt road to an elevation of 7,750 feet next to the Pine Marten knob, a prominent lava cone near the lodge. The project required transporting 22,000 bolts, 320,000 pounds of rebar and around 600 truckloads of concrete up to the site. At one point, about 150 workers were on the project site.

During the final month of construction, as winter neared, workers used Sno-Cats to reach the site. They completed the thirty-seven-thousand-square-foot lodge on time and at a cost of $4.5 million. In the end, the design process took three months and construction, six months. Once completed, the lodge featured a gourmet dining room and spectacular views of South Sister and Broken Top. The project received an award from *World of Concrete* magazine in recognition of its technical complexity and degree of difficulty.[148]

THE CHANGING OF THE OLD GUARD AND SLOWING GROWTH

Bill Healy remained focused on many other projects critical to Mt. Bachelor's future despite his declining health. These included construction of a new guest services building, an improved radio communications system, computerized ticketing services, new grooming equipment, upgrades to food and rental services and expanded parking.

Healy continued working closely with the local business community, promoting Bend's tourism economy. He served as a board member and early promoter of the Central Oregon Recreation Association, later called the Central Oregon Visitors Association.[149] In that role, Healy focused on projects making it easier for tourists to reach Central Oregon, such as offering charter bus service from the Redmond airport and a shuttle linking the Amtrak station in Chemult, Oregon, to Bend for skiers arriving by train from California.

Healy also began a newspaper advertising campaign in major West Coast markets promoting Central Oregon tourism. One season, the marketing strategy even included an ill-fated effort to prepurchase airline seats, meant to incentivize airlines to book more wintertime direct flights into Redmond.[150]

During this period, there were several changes to the board of directors. In 1983, Felix Marcoulier, one of the original board members, sold his remaining shares to Dean Papé. This left Healy and Dr. Bradford Pease as the last remaining original board members.[151] Then, in 1988, Healy was hospitalized with a concussion and a broken hip after a wheelchair accident. This incident prompted Healy to step back from his role as president of Mt. Bachelor Inc., moving David Marsh into the position.

Healy's declining health soon forced a more dramatic reshuffling of Mt. Bachelor's senior leadership.[152] In July 1988, Mt. Bachelor's majority shareholders (Healy, Papé, Pease, McClain and the Stevenson family) announced a plan to purchase all outstanding public shares and place them under a new corporation. Most of the shares in question were held by community members, including many of Mt. Bachelor's original investors.

The proposal caused an uproar among shareholders who felt undercut by the sudden change.[153] The board's main argument in favor of the proposal was that the new arrangement would streamline financial reporting and protect the corporation from outside takeover. That didn't alleviate bad feelings in the community over how the board had handled the transaction.

As the 1980s ended, Mt. Bachelor closed out a decade of rapid growth, unprecedented investment and significant infrastructure development. The 1988–89 season delivered another banner year, with nearly 650,000 skier visits. The resort was, by then, well established as a regional destination and was fast becoming a world-class ski area. After years of breakneck expansion, the new decade began a period of slower growth with more limited ambitions. The 1989–90 season saw a delayed opening due to poor weather and financial losses relating to the air charter scheme that suffered from a lack of guests.

Despite a drop-off in visitor numbers, the company continued moving forward with several projects to improve the guest experience. These included automated ticketing and a telephone reservations system. The old guest services building was renovated to provide locker rooms and space for ticket operations. Work began on a new retail and rental center in the West Village base area. Plans included a much-needed expansion of Century Drive between Sunriver Junction and the Mt. Bachelor base area, expanding the highway from two to four lanes.

The 1993 season was one of triumph and tragedy. The year kicked off Mt. Bachelor's most extensive lift construction effort since its founding, an investment of $2.7 million in three new lifts. The project included replacing the original Sunrise triple Yan with a new Doppelmayr high-speed quad. Parts from the old Sunrise lift were repurposed as the Alpenglow lift, providing improved access to beginner terrain from the Sunrise base area. Finally, the Little Pine lift, a Doppelmayr high-speed quad with a capacity of 2,200 skiers per hour, was built in place of the Orange Chair. The new equipment brought the mountain's overall lift capacity to over 22,000 skiers per hour.[154]

Unfortunately, Healy didn't live to see the projects through to completion. In October of that year, he passed away from complications of Lou Gehrig's disease.[155] At the end of that season, the mountain closed with almost six hundred thousand skier visits, placing it in the ranks of the top ski resorts in the United States and vindicating Healy's grand vision for Mt. Bachelor.

Shortly before his death, Healy had been named an honorary captain of the U.S. Olympic biathlon team for the games in Albertville, Canada. That was followed by numerous other tributes to his achievements. In 1997, Mt. Bachelor dedicated a bronze statue of Healy outside the Pine Marten Lodge. The ceremony included members of the local skiing community and many of Healy's former comrades from the Tenth Mountain Division. In 1998, he was posthumously inducted into the Northwest Ski Hall of Fame and was made an honorary member of the National Ski Patrol, among other recognitions.

In 2003, the Bend City Council voted unanimously to name a new bridge spanning the Deschutes River the Bill Healy Memorial Bridge.[156] During the dedication ceremony, city officials noted that Bend would not have achieved its place as a thriving tourism destination without Healy's vision and determination to create the ski area. More recently, in 2019, the Mt. Bachelor Sports Education Foundation (MBSEF) named its new training facility after Healy. The facility was built, in part, through a pledge from the Healy Foundation, creating a center for Central Oregon youth pursuing personal growth through winter sports.

After Healy's passing, the company's leadership, under Papé and Marsh, continued pursuing his vision by investing in new equipment, services and

Bill Healy with Mt. Bachelor in the background. *Sketch by Dave Adamson, courtesy of Mt. Bachelor Sports Education Foundation.*

facilities. In 1996, the company launched the decade's last major lift upgrade with the new Northwest Express chair. The Doppelmayr high-speed quad had a capacity of 2,800 skiers per hour and the highest vertical climb of any lift on the mountain. As the westernmost lift on the mountain, it opened over 450 acres of new terrain and ten runs. That same year, the Summit Express was converted to a Doppelmayr high-speed quad with a capacity of 2,800 skiers per hour.

Despite the new upgrades, Mt. Bachelor entered a period of flattening growth during the 1990s, with annual skier visits plateauing at around 500,000. The decade ended with approximately 460,000 skier visits in 1999, down almost 15 percent from the previous season and delivering the company's first net loss in several years.[157] Slowing growth forced the board to reevaluate the projections it had used in the 1980 master plan to reach one million skier visits per year. However, the rising popularity of snowboarding was drawing a new demographic to the resort as skier numbers declined. By the early 2000s, snowboarders represented around one-fifth of all guests coming to the resort.[158]

In the years after Healy's passing, the remaining original board members eventually relinquished their roles. Dr. Pease retired and passed his seat to his son, Norman Pease. Dean Papé died in 1996 following a medical procedure, and his seat went to his son Randy. David Marsh, who had worked his way up the management ladder, was still serving as president and CEO. However, Marsh retired suddenly in 1998 and died several years later from cancer.[159] After Marsh retired, Randy Papé became president and general manager.

With Healy's death and the last members of the original board no longer serving, the end of the 1990s marked the passing of Mt. Bachelor's founding generation. Starting in 1958 with limited resources, they had built a nationally known resort providing a skier experience unlike anywhere else in the United States. Their achievement was even more impressive because of how they did it. From the beginning, Mt. Bachelor remained a local enterprise, funded primarily by Central Oregonians and led by community members.

Under Healy's leadership, Mt. Bachelor became a vehicle of economic transformation that turned a dying logging town into a destination for outdoor tourism, creating new opportunities for residents. He built a highly regarded ski area that became a top training destination for world-class athletes. As the resort grew, Healy often placed local interests before profits, ensuring that Mt. Bachelor's success worked to improve prospects for the entire community. While the new century would bring a significant transition in the resort's ownership and management, Healy's legacy would continue to impact the mountain and the community for generations.

CHAPTER 5

NEW OWNERSHIP AND MODERNIZATION

M t. Bachelor's next decade began amid controversy concerning some board members' desire to sell the resort. The news created a schism on the board and among many longtime shareholders. The proposal came as the ski industry was undergoing significant transformation and consolidation. During Mt. Bachelor's era of rapid expansion in the 1970s and '80s, many smaller ski areas went out of business. Some, like Mt. Bachelor, survived by expanding, while ski conglomerates purchased others.

Industry statistics provide a vivid picture of the transformation. According to the National Ski Areas Association, in the late 1960s, around 1,400 ski areas were operating in the United States. By the mid-1970s, that number had dropped to 930. Twenty years later, the number was closer to 500.[160] However, even as the number of resorts declined, overall skier capacity gradually increased through investments in infrastructure, services and amenities that drew in new customers.

Nationally, annual skier visits expanded around 1.2 percent annually during the first decade of the 2000s.[161] With industry growth flatlined, many resorts sought new sources of revenue from services, amenities, real estate development and expansion to four-season operations. That business strategy involved a process of vertical integration at destination resorts like Vail and Whistler/Blackcomb, where skiers spent more money off the slopes than on. This was not the development model adopted by resorts like Mt. Bachelor and other ski areas in Oregon.

Nearly all Oregon's ski resorts operated under special-use permits on national forest lands. With this came significant limitations on base area development. That legacy encouraged the growth of "gateway towns" clustered around Oregon ski areas rather than the development of high-density slope-side amenities and lodging. One 2012 industry survey found that nearly 80 percent of skier visits to Oregon resorts were "day visits" rather than "destination visits."[162] The same study noted that destination skiers were spending more than three times as much as day skiers per visit.

Industry trends were moving away from the development model embraced by Bill Healy and Mt. Bachelor's founders. With major resorts focusing on improving the customer experience by offering a wider variety of activities and amenities, there was a sense that Mt. Bachelor was falling behind its competitors.[163] Making matters worse, Mt. Bachelor's shareholders had ended the 1999–2000 season facing a significant downturn in skier visits and two consecutive years of financial losses.[164] In the spring of 2001, the board of directors and shareholders received an offer from the Utah-based Powdr Corporation to buy the resort.

THE START OF A NEW ERA

Powdr Corp was founded in 1994 by Ian Cumming and his son John. Ian was a successful real estate developer, investment banker and philanthropist who died in 2018. Before becoming involved with Powdr, the younger Cumming had cofounded the outdoor clothing company Mountain Hardwear in 1993 with several former employees of Sierra Designs. Before that, he worked as a guide for Rainier Mountaineering.[165] Mountain Hardwear's first sponsored athlete was Ed Viesturs, the first American to climb all fourteen 8,000-meter peaks. Viesturs played an active role in product design and promoting the brand's high-performance climbing gear. In 2003, the Portland-based Columbia Sportswear acquired the company.

Before starting Powdr, John Cumming spent several years learning about the ski industry from Nick Badami, the majority shareholder of Alpine Meadows of Tahoe Inc., owner of the Park City and Alpine Meadows ski areas. John Cumming later served as Powdr's first president, with his brother David as vice president and Nick Badami as board chairman. In the first year of operation, the company acquired controlling stock in Alpine Meadows of California and gained ownership over Park City Mountain Resort in Utah. The company acquired Boreal Mountain and Soda Springs in California the following year.[166]

John Cumming was familiar with Mt. Bachelor from previous visits. After skiing there in 1996, he told resort president David Marsh that he wanted to buy it. Cumming reportedly called Mount Bachelor "the most beautiful place I ever skied."[167] When Cumming learned that the company might be up for sale, Powdr approached shareholders with an offer.[168]

At the time, the Papé Group was Mount Bachelor's largest shareholder, holding around 23 percent of the 1,382 total shares. Randy Papé, president of the Eugene-based Papé Group, also served as president and board member of Mt. Bachelor Inc. Members of the Healy family held the second-largest block, with control over 17 percent of the shares. The Stevenson family of Bingen, Washington, was the remaining major shareholder.[169]

Powdr initially offered shareholders $20,100 per share plus free lifetime skiing at all company-owned ski resorts to close the deal. The offer revealed differing perspectives among board members and shareholders concerned about Mt. Bachelor's future direction. Randy Papé and the board promptly rejected the initial offer, with Wallace Stevenson reportedly being the only board member in favor of the deal.

In a January 2001 letter to shareholders, Papé expressed concern about relinquishing ownership to "out-of-state interests."[170] However, he acknowledged that the corporation was facing a year of disappointing financial performance due to changing market dynamics and unfavorable weather conditions.

Despite the board's opposition, shareholders were divided over the best course of action, with the Healy family leaning toward accepting Powdr's offer. In an interview with the *Bulletin*, Papé said he believed that Mt. Bachelor could remain a stand-alone entity while competing against the large resort conglomerates.[171] He believed that skiers would be better served by maintaining local ownership while developing Mt. Bachelor into a destination resort by adding year-round recreational experiences, new snowmaking capabilities, night skiing and lodging. At the time, Papé described Mt. Bachelor as an "overgrown day operation," with the lift capacity of a destination resort but none of the amenities.[172]

In January 2001, the board met to review the offer and provide a nonbinding recommendation to shareholders. The Papé Group made a competing offer the following month, ranging from $22,100 to $25,000 per share. However, at the time, most shareholders had decided to accept Powdr's offer, according to media reports. Consequently, the board of directors voted to waive a state statute that would have prevented the sale as part of a hostile takeover.[173] That decision prompted a lawsuit by Papé Group, charging that the board had breached its fiduciary duties by agreeing to waive the law restricting the takeover.

As part of a settlement agreement, the board recommended that shareholders accept the Papé Group's offer. Shareholders were free to accept or reject that recommendation. By the end of March, most shareholders had already pledged or sold their stock to Powdr. Shortly after the board's decision, the Healy family, holding 17 percent of outstanding shares, reaffirmed their desire to accept Powdr's offer. The deal closed for around $28 million, giving Powdr nearly 70 percent of outstanding shares and ownership of Mt. Bachelor.

As the new owner, John Cumming wasted no time reaching out to the community. He expressed his desire to work with local business leaders to improve marketing and attract more out-of-town overnight skiers.[174] He also pledged to invest in snowmaking equipment and to consider offering night skiing. As part of the transfer in ownership, Dan Rutherford, the former vice president, replaced Randy Papé as general manager. In September that year, the Forest Service issued a new forty-year permit to Mt. Bachelor LLC.

After the deal closed, the new owners began trimming costs to bring operations back to profitability. Management ranks were cut nearly in half, along with additional reductions in seasonal staff. However, there were also concerns over how Powdr's management planned to reverse Mt. Bachelor's recent financial losses. There were some accusations in the media that Powdr intended to bring in foreign workers at lower wages.[175] The resort dropped its free skiing program for local sixth graders and shortened the spring season to save money.[176] Other cost-cutting measures included selling Mt. Bachelor's office building in Bend and a park-and-ride lot.

Annual skier visits remained relatively stable during the first five years under new ownership, hovering around five hundred thousand. However, the company reported a significant increase in adjusted gross revenues: approximately 21 percent.[177] That jump occurred even though skier visits increased by only 3 percent over the same period. Some critics suggested that the resort's financial turnaround came at the expense of longtime customers now paying more for season passes. Other observers accused Powdr of shortchanging safety and infrastructure investments as a strategy for boosting profits.

At the same time, the company was moving forward with several significant investments that were part of the existing master plan. In 2002, Powdr purchased an SMI snowmaking system covering the Thunderbird run, the terrain park and the half-pipe, allowing for early season snowmaking.[178] In

2006, Powdr invested $3.5 million in upgrading the Pine Marten Express to a Doppelmayr high-speed quad. Other upgrades included a complete renovation of the West Village Lodge, new snowcats and a modernized ticketing system. The resort also maintained some money-losing programs, such as operating a skier shuttle bus from Bend.

Elements of Powdr's strategy reflected changing dynamics across the industry. As the sport matured, lift tickets represented a shrinking portion of overall ski area revenues. In the mid-1970s, ticket sales generated around 80 percent of revenue for the average ski area. Since then, that number has dropped by half, with more revenue coming from services, food and beverages, lessons, accommodations, property development and retail sales.[179] With fewer on-slope amenities and no overnight accommodations, Mt. Bachelor had to rely on ticket sales, proximity to a sizable customer base and reliable snow conditions to sustain profitability.[180]

After several years under the new ownership, the strategy appeared to be working. The 2005–6 season was the resort's second-best on record, with around 590,000 skier visits. However, the following year saw around a 10 percent drop in visitors because of poor weather, returning to the longer-term average.[181] At the same time, media reports suggested a perception among local skiers of frustration with the resort's operations and services.[182]

The 2006–7 season brought more of the same. Mt. Bachelor saw a 7 percent drop in skier visits during a year when other Oregon ski areas reported record-breaking numbers. During the 2007–8 season, Mt. Hood Meadows attracted more annual visitors than Mt. Bachelor for the first time.[183] Mt. Bachelor was also losing customers to resorts in British Columbia and Washington State, with a sharp drop-off in skiers arriving from Seattle.[184]

Beyond declining skier numbers, Powdr was going through a significant turnover with its leadership at Mt. Bachelor. In 2007, Dan Rutherford resigned as president and general manager. Rutherford had been employed at Mt. Bachelor since 1971 and had served as president since 2002. He was replaced by Matt Janney, who had worked at Mt. Bachelor from 1977 to 2003 in various positions, including lift operations manager and director of operations. Janney previously led Powdr's Lake Tahoe–area properties at Alpine Meadows, Boreal Mountain and Soda Springs.

However, Janney's tenure at Mt. Bachelor lasted only ten months. In the summer of 2008, Powdr replaced Janney as general manager, along with the directors of marketing, food and beverage services and operations.[185] Janney was succeeded by Dave Rathbun, who had previously served as vice president of marketing and sales at Killington Resort and Pico Mountain in Vermont, both Powdr-owned properties.[186]

At the time of the leadership change, the company acknowledged challenges with equipment maintenance, lift operations and community relations. From 2005 to 2010, the resort saw a declining trend in overall visits.[187] During the 1980s, Mt. Bachelor had averaged close to six hundred thousand annual skier days, but in the early 2000s, this number dropped off to the high four hundred thousands.[188] Visitor numbers at the Nordic Center showed a similar trend, averaging between ten and eighteen thousand guests per year, down from their high point in the early 1990s.

To reverse the trend, Rathbun's team began finalizing an updated master development plan (MDP), the ski area's first formal submission to the Forest Service since 1987.[189] The plan had several overarching goals focused on rebalancing capacity, modernizing facilities and adapting the resort to changing skier preferences.[190]

At the time of the update, the resort was operating twelve lifts with a total operational capacity of 23,050 passengers per hour, servicing eighty-nine groomed runs and a Nordic network consisting of fifty-six kilometers covering twelve named trails. However, several aspects of the existing infrastructure were negatively impacting customer experience, such as an imbalance between trail and lift capacity and a lack of beginner facilities and terrain. Additionally, customers perceived the resort's lodge areas and services to be outdated.

Ecosign Mountain Resort Planners was selected to prepare the MDP, with Cirrus Ecological Solutions working on the environmental impact statement.[191] The final MDP outlined several specific objectives. The first involved significant improvements to the Sunrise base area. Concerns for this area included the underutilization of the Rainbow Chair due to its slow operating speed. The report also noted problems with overcrowding at Sunrise Lodge and a lack of parking.

The proposed plan involved developing a new east side express lift and associated trails while lowering the catchline to provide additional areas for tree skiing. The east side express would open a larger area of low intermediate–to intermediate-level terrain on the eastern edge of the ski area. It also included several new trails in the lower Rainbow area. These developments were particularly important on inclement weather days, when the summit chair and west side lifts were often closed due to high winds. Another objective involved reorganizing the Sunrise base area with an expansion of the day lodge, more parking and the addition of several beginner lifts.

The MDP also included plans for development on the resort's western side. The proposals included additional guest parking, expansion of the West Village Lodge and a new cross-country learning area closer to the Nordic lodge. Other proposals involved continued expansion of terrain parks and features appealing to snowboarders, who represented around 30 percent of the resort's ticket sales.

Another key element of the MDP involved expanding the range of summer activities, an area in which the resort lagged its competitors. In 2010–11, despite a record-breaking seasonal snowfall of 665 inches at Mt. Bachelor, Mt. Hood Skibowl drew more annual visitors than Mt. Bachelor for the first time. This was attributed, in part, to Skibowl's expansion of summertime activities such as lift-served mountain biking, a luge ride, bungee jumping and special events.[192]

Mt. Bachelor's push to expand its four-season operations reflected a broader trend across the industry. One impetus for this change was the Ski Area Recreational Opportunity Enhancement Act, passed by Congress in 2011. The new legislation amended the National Forest Ski Area Permit Act of 1986, which had previously limited resorts' ability to develop infrastructure for summer recreation.[193]

This change cleared the way for expansion of summer activities as the industry faced two existential threats. The first of these was from the long-term stagnation of skier numbers and the aging of the sport's customer base. Expansion into year-round activities offered resorts a path toward offsetting declining skier numbers. A second factor was the longer-term concern over climate change, with many lower-elevation resorts facing the likelihood of shorter winter seasons and less predictable snowpack.[194]

The legislative changes applied to the 122 ski areas around the county operating on national forest land. It opened the door for new amenities such as zip lines, mountain bike terrain parks, trails and frisbee golf courses. Many ski areas took advantage of the new rules to expand such offerings. According to industry research, between 2009 and 2014, summer visitation at U.S. ski resorts grew by 37 percent.[195]

Mt. Bachelor's new MDP reflected this trend, proposing several activities to increase summertime recreational options. These included using the Pine Marten lift for sightseeing trips and dining at the mid-mountain lodge. The plan also called for hiking trails centered on the Pine Marten Lodge and lift-serviced downhill mountain biking. Finally, the MDP envisioned a zip line tour dropping from the Pine Marten Lodge to the West Village base area. The concepts aligned with Powdr's broader strategy of diversifying beyond snow sports and rebranding itself as an "adventure lifestyle company."

In 2013, the Forest Service signed its Record of Decision approving Mt. Bachelor's ten-year MDP. This included plans to accommodate as many as twenty-six thousand visitors per day with several options for expanding year-round recreation and cleared the way for developing a downhill mountain bike park, zip line tours and a new east side quad lift. It also allowed for the replacement of the Rainbow and Sunrise lifts, renovation of the Sunrise Lodge and expansion of the east side parking area.[196]

Mt. Bachelor was one of many resorts developing lift-serviced downhill mountain biking as part of their four-season strategies. The resort worked with Gravity Logic, an internationally known team that helped design Canada's Whistler Mountain Bike Park. The proposal called for a trail system extending from the mountain's northwest to northeast, taking advantage of its unique volcanic topography. The first phase of the bike park began in 2013, and it gradually grew into a network offering thirteen miles of lift-served single track.

In the summer of 2016, the resort began construction of its first new lift in twenty years since the opening of Northwest Express in 1996. Dubbed Cloudchaser, the Doppelmayr high-speed detachable quad cost $6.5 million and had a capacity of 2,400 skiers per hour. The lift opened 635 acres of new terrain, covering thirteen new runs on the mountain's northeastern side. The new area increased the resort's total skiable terrain to 4,318 acres, making Mt. Bachelor the sixth-largest ski resort in the United States.

After opening the Cloudchaser lift, the resort continued development around the eastside base area. This included a major renovation of Sunrise Lodge with improved restrooms, a rental shop and a food court. A third parking lot adjacent to the Sunrise base area increased parking capacity by 50 percent. It improved access by adding a new 629-foot quad chairlift named Early Riser, serving five acres of beginner terrain below Sunrise Lodge.[197]

In 2016, Powdr expanded its summer recreation portfolio by purchasing Bend-based Sun Country Tours. The company was founded in 1978 by Dennis Oliphant, a former college ski racer and an early employee of Mt. Bachelor's Nordic Center. Sun Country's business focused on rafting trips along the Deschutes, North Umpqua and McKenzie Rivers, stand-up paddleboarding and tubing.[198] The Sun Country acquisition allowed Mt. Bachelor to expand its summer programs while consolidating customer booking between the two entities. Many seasonal employees traditionally moved between the two businesses; therefore, the merger offered streamlined operations and personnel management.

With a continuing focus on expanding year-round operations, in 2020, the resort opened its long-awaited zip line. With a total length of 1.3 miles, the zip line was constructed in three stages. The first stage starts near the Pine Marten lift and descends 255 feet, offering views of nearby Tumalo Mountain and Paulina Peak to the east. The second stage drops 263 feet, and the final, longest stage covers over 3,400 feet with an 866-foot vertical drop, offering dramatic views of Broken Top.[199]

Continuing its expansion of summer offerings, in 2021, Mt. Bachelor announced plans to develop a new hiking and mountain biking trail circling the mountain's base and climbing to the summit.[200] The proposed hiking route would link the Pine Marten Lodge to the summit and return to the West Village base near the Outback chairlift. Plans for the hiking trail include historical landmarks and interpretive signs.

CHAPTER 6

MOUNT BACHELOR AND THE U.S. FOREST SERVICE

An important part of Mount Bachelor's story involves the close relationship between the ski area and the U.S. Forest Service. This collaboration was instrumental to the resort's establishment and throughout its development. Since Bachelor Butte was located within the Deschutes National Forest, Bill Healy understood that it was critical to have support from the Forest Service to realize his vision. Several members of the Forest Service played vital roles in moving the project from site selection through the early phases of development.

In 1957, after a fire severely damaged the Skyliners facilities above Tumalo Creek, club members set out to find a new location for the ski hill. Two Forest Service employees, Don Peters and Ed Parker, joined Bill Healy, Gene Gillis and several other Skyliners members on missions to scout locations. After several weeks of touring the high country and considering various sites, the group was unanimous that Bachelor Butte was the ideal spot.[201]

Healy and Gillis began sketching an initial concept while soliciting Forest Service support to move the plan forward. James Egan, the new Deschutes National Forest supervisor, joined a group of boosters for a survey trip to the proposed location. After touring the area, Egan was convinced that Bachelor Butte offered a "thrilling location for a winter sports center, with its fine snow and its grand view of the Cascades."[202]

Don Peters was Egan's staff officer in charge of recreation. He was a Skyliners member and an early advocate for moving the club's activities up to Bachelor Butte. As the plan progressed, Peters played an essential role in facilitating the environmental study and permitting aspects of the proposal. This process was no small matter and involved a complete environmental assessment, archaeological survey and impact study of the proposed site.

The Forest Service required that ski resorts operating under special-use permits develop detailed plans for funding, liability insurance, environmental protection and provisions for ski patrol and first aid. Given Bachelor Butte's somewhat remote location, twenty miles from Bend, the Forest Service also required plans for constructing an access road to the base area and capabilities for snow removal. Healy had to resolve all these details before receiving approval to move ahead.

The permit application required Healy and his backers to make an economic case demonstrating that the enterprise would be financially viable. One of the original board members, Dr. Bradford Pease, wrote a letter to the Forest Service, assuring it that a ski area would draw enough visitors to justify the investment. The Bend Chamber of Commerce and other local boosters endorsed the letter.

While Egan personally supported the idea, he was obligated to inform Pease and Healy that much work had to be done before a permit could be approved. In addition to building the access road and providing for snow removal, Healy needed to ensure that the base area had water supply and sanitation, a parking area, lifts and lodge facilities.

Egan noted that the Forest Service Pacific Northwest Region office in Portland was less than enthusiastic about the proposal.[203] Its primary concern was that Bachelor Butte wouldn't draw enough skiers from outside Central Oregon, given that the Mount Hood and Hoodoo Bowl ski areas were already well established.

Don Peters, the Deschutes National Forest staff officer in charge of recreation, became Healy's strongest advocate within the Forest Service, making the case for Bachelor Butte. Peters gathered all the information needed to convince the agency's regional office in Portland and headquarters in Washington, D.C., and then prepared an endorsement letter for Egan's signature. Meanwhile, Healy continued working on the other permit requirements, such as obtaining liability insurance, making plans for clearing the base area and ordering equipment for the lifts.

Building and paying for the access road was another obstacle where Peters and Egan proved instrumental. The two men worked with the Deschutes County commissioners on an arrangement whereby the Forest Service would design the road and reimburse the county for snow removal based on receipts from the ski area. While this was happening, Peters oversaw the

Plaque from the Egan Lodge dedicated to Deschutes National Forest supervisor James Egan. *Photo by Glenn Voelz, courtesy of Ray Brooks.*

environmental assessment and site studies required by the Forest Service. Peters also worked closely with Gene Gillis on the site development plan, including recommending the location for the first rope tows and selecting the equipment.

Nothing epitomized the close partnership between Bachelor Butte and the Forest Service more than the naming of the original ski lodge. When the building was dedicated in January 1959, several months after the ski area opened, it was named in honor of James Egan, the Deschutes National Forest supervisor. Egan had started with the Forest Service in 1935 and served in the navy during World War II. Tragically, he died of leukemia in early 1958 at the age of forty-five and didn't live to see the resort open.

Arguably, the relationship between Healy and the Forest Service may have been overly close by modern ethical standards. As a government employee, Don Peters spent much of his off-duty time consulting for Healy during the early days of the enterprise. Peters had previously worked on ski area permitting and safety issues in other parts of Oregon and Washington State. Therefore, he was familiar with what was required to move the Bachelor Butte proposal through the Forest Service bureaucracy.

Healy told historian Peggy Chessman Lucas that Mt. Bachelor was born from a close collaborative effort among private citizens, local government and the Forest Service. He joked that they probably "broke a few rules" to get the project going.[204] This is not to say that the Forest Service always gave Healy a blank check for everything he wanted. There were numerous instances in which the Forest Service disapproved of Healy's plans or required modifications to his proposals.

The ski area's original opening date in late 1957 was delayed for a season, allowing time for the Forest Service to complete its surveys for the special-use permit. In 1965, before opening the new base area lodge, Don Peters discovered a problem with the sewage disposal system that could have carried effluent into the porous lava rock, contaminating the water table and potentially affecting the city's watershed. As required, Peters reported the problem to the Oregon office of sanitation and engineering, delaying the lodge's opening until the following season, much to Healy's frustration.[205]

The Forest Service also denied Mt. Bachelor's proposal for accessing water from a meadow above Todd Lake using a pipeline running across Dutchman Flat, which would have supplied the resort with up to seventy thousand gallons of water per day.[206] The agency cited potential damage to the sensitive riparian ecosystem along Todd Creek. Again, during the master planning process in the late 1970s, the Forest Service disallowed several proposals based on its environmental assessment, initially objecting to an access road needed to build the proposed summit lift. The Forest Service's overriding concern was the potential visual impact on scenery when melting snow exposed the scarred landscape during the summer months.[207]

The Forest Service also sided with community leaders concerned about increased traffic congestion on Century Drive. In its planning documents, Mt. Bachelor had used an unrealistic assumption about the number of skiers that would travel to the resort by bus and carpool.[208] Healy worked with the Forest Service and the Department of Transportation to find a compromise involving widening portions of Century Drive, creating chain-up areas and encouraging skiers to use buses.

After the ski area opened, Don Peters continued working closely with Mt. Bachelor as a Forest Service employee over the next two decades. Peters was responsible for inspecting the facilities and ensuring safety standards. This included performing structural inspections of the chairlifts and ensuring the readiness and training of the ski patrol. Peters even received an award from the National Ski Patrol for a 1958 rescue involving renowned local skier Terry Skjersaa, who was seriously injured while skiing on the mountain.[209]

The Forest Service maintained a full-time snow ranger at Bachelor Butte during its early years of operation. Initially, the job was much more hands-on than administrative. Ray Bennet, who was Mt. Bachelor's first snow ranger, previously worked at Steamboat Spring and understood the business of skiing. Dave Rasmussen came on in 1961 as the resort's second snow ranger. He was a Bend local who had grown up skiing at Hoodoo before joining the Forest Service.[210]

Rasmussen served in the position of snow ranger for ten years and spent much of his time monitoring safety and operations while on skis. He functioned as the main liaison between the resort and the Deschutes National Forest. Rasmussen's duties included daily equipment inspections, monitoring avalanche safety, ski patrol training and public relations with visitors. The Forest Service was also responsible for approving operational hours and monitoring health and safety protocols.

Deschutes National Forest snow ranger Dave Rasmussen on duty, January 1965. *Photo by Walter Meyer. Deschutes National Forest.*

As the ski industry matured and professionalized, resort operators gradually assumed many snow ranger responsibilities. However, the Forest Service continued monitoring regulatory compliance and safety. Today, the Deschutes National Forest has specific responsibilities for administering the special-use permit. These include ensuring compliance with all permit conditions and existing laws, regulations and policies.

Mt. Bachelor, like most large resorts, handles daily avalanche mitigation. However, the Forest Service assists in evaluating avalanche hazards and monitoring control efforts. This is done in conjunction with the Forest Service National Avalanche Center. The center provides expertise to its field units, conducts avalanche education, helps transfer new technologies to the field and facilitates avalanche research on behalf of the Forest Service.[211]

The Forest Service also monitors structures and facilities for compliance with safety requirements. It helps the resort evaluate potential hazards, assists with risk mitigation, monitors weather conditions and develops guidelines for lift operations, ski runs and signage.[212] Additionally, the Forest Service maintains a visible public presence on the mountain, where naturalists offer interpretive tours discussing the area's winter ecology, geology and flora and fauna.

THE EVOLUTION OF THE FOREST SERVICE'S ROLE IN OUTDOOR RECREATION

The Forest Service's involvement in outdoor recreation reflects a long-term evolution in its approach to land management. When Congress created the Forest Service in 1905, the agency's focus was on maximizing the economic value of lands under its purview. This priority was a direct legacy of the 1897 Organic Act, which authorized the establishment of national forest reserves to "furnish a continuous supply of timber for the use and necessities of the people of the United States."[213] This directive reflected an economic-use philosophy central to the government's early land management practices. In Central Oregon and other areas of the West, this primarily meant managing land for grazing and timber production.

At that time, the government didn't consider recreation a highly productive use of forest lands. Under the Forest Service's first chief, Gifford Pinchot, the newly created agency focused on managing forest resources based on "the greatest good of the greatest number for the longest time."[214] However, Pinchot also recognized the potential for the national forests to "serve a good purpose as great playgrounds for the people."[215]

Before World War I, recreation on national forest land was mainly unmonitored and generally limited to hunting, fishing and camping. But as more Americans gained access to automobiles, they began exploring national forest lands for recreation. In 1917, the Forest Service conducted its first comprehensive recreation study on national forest lands.[216] It hired

Frank Waugh, a noted professor of landscape architecture, to conduct the study. Waugh spent nearly six months doing fieldwork across the county, providing a definitive survey of campgrounds, resorts and other recreational facilities on national forest lands.

Waugh's report provided the first analysis of recreation-use statistics and placed a direct economic value on these activities. Perhaps most importantly, Waugh argued that recreation should be placed on equal footing with other land-use priorities such as timber production and grazing. He noted in his report that "outdoor recreation is a necessity of civilized life, and as civilization becomes more intensive, the demand grows keener."[217] Waugh's report encouraged the Forest Service to include recreational planning as part of its land management responsibilities, which led to improvements in services, facilities and sanitation.

In 1916, the Forest Service built its first campground and trail system designed specifically for recreational use, at Eagle Creek in the Columbia River Gorge.[218] This area became the prototype for today's national forest campgrounds by offering designated campsites with water, tables and toilets. That same year, President Woodrow Wilson created the National Park Service, setting aside some of the nation's more scenic lands exclusively for preservation and recreation.[219] Around the same time, the Deschutes National Forest published its first forest recreation plan.[220]

The following year, Frederick Cleator, one of the Forest Service's first recreational planners, arrived at his new assignment in the Portland regional office. One of his major tasks, starting in 1920, was charting the route for a scenic driving road through the High Cascades between Mount Hood and Crater Lake. Although the proposed highway turned out to be infeasible, the route Cleator developed eventually became the Oregon Skyline Trail, one of the nation's earliest long-distance hiking trails and the inspiration for naming Bend's Skyliners ski club.[221] Sections of that route are now incorporated into the Pacific Crest National Scenic Trail.

Cleator also played an important role in planning and designing sites for recreational use during the 1920s.[222] As a result of the Term Occupancy Permit Act of 1915, the Forest Service began permitting recreational infrastructure inside national forest lands, such as campgrounds, summer homes and concessionaire-operated resorts.[223] During the 1920s, the Forest Service issued thousands of permits for recreational residences across Oregon and Washington, including over 280 in the Deschutes National Forest.

In the late 1920s, thirty-two permits were issued for residences around Elk Lake.[224] Early Skyliners member Paul Hosmer received one of the

OREGON
SKYLINE TRAIL
1936

PACIFIC
CREST SYSTEM
U. S. DEPT. OF AGRICULTURE
FOREST SERVICE
REGION-6
GUIDE NO. 35 OREGON

Cover of the Oregon Skyline Trail guide, circa 1936. *Oregon Historical Society.*

first permits to build a family cabin on the shores of the lake. Around the same time, Alan Wilcoxson received a permit to build a lodge and resort at Elk Lake. By the end of the 1920s, the site was a popular summer recreation spot, hosting a "yacht club" for boaters and offering cabins for rent along Elk Creek.

By the early 1930s, with the many competing demands for forest lands, Congress ordered a detailed study of forestry policy in the United States. The result was a 1,677-page study known as the Copeland Report. The report addressed all aspects of forestry policy, including recreation, and became the blueprint for transforming national forest lands under the New Deal.[225]

Robert Marshall, who would later become the Forest Service's first chief of recreation and lands, wrote a chapter of the Copeland Report focused entirely on recreation. Under Marshall's leadership, the Forest Service massively expanded the agency's recreational infrastructure, allowing for the development of many of the nation's first ski resorts on national forest land.

Around half of the sixty-some ski areas developed in the United States between the two World Wars were on national forest lands. In Oregon, these included the Cooper Spur and Skibowl areas on Mount Hood, opened in the late 1920s, Timberline in 1937, Hoodoo in 1938 and Willamette Pass in 1941.

After the World War II, recreational visits to the national forests surged from around eighteen to fifty-three million per year.[226] This led the Forest Service to focus more attention on developing new recreational infrastructure. In 1948, Forest Service employee Wilfred "Slim" Davis conducted the first comprehensive survey of national forest lands considered most suitable for development as ski areas.[227] Like many of his

Early campers at Elk Lake with Bachelor Butte in the background. *Deschutes County Historical Society.*

contemporaries, Davis was a lifelong skier and Tenth Mountain Division veteran. He became instrumental in developing numerous ski areas during his forty-year career in the Forest Service.

As developers looked to build new resorts, much of the best ski terrain in the western United States was located on federal lands.[228] During early westward expansion and settlement, these rugged, remote areas were considered less economically valuable and thus remained undeveloped. Between the end of World War II and 1960, around thirty new ski areas were built on national forest lands, including Whitefish, Squaw Valley, Mammoth, Taos, Heavenly, Solitude, Aspen and Mt. Bachelor.

Given the growing interest in outdoor recreation, Congress created the Outdoor Recreation Resources Review Commission in 1958 to analyze how the government managed these activities.[229] The study resulted in the 1962 report *Outdoor Recreation for America*, which recommended that the federal government take a leading role in preserving scenic areas, primitive wilderness and historic sites. The report also urged the government to manage federal lands for the broadest possible recreational benefit consistent with other essential uses.[230]

Within the National Forest System, the Multiple-Use Sustained-Yield Act of 1960 reflected these changing values, including the growing importance of recreation on public lands. The legislation grew out of concerns about the detrimental impacts of logging and water reclamation projects inside the national forests. Notably, the act placed activities such as recreation and conservation on equal footing with traditional uses like timber production and grazing. Furthermore, it explicitly defined "multiple uses" to include outdoor recreation as a function that would best meet and serve human needs.[231]

In practical terms, the multiple-use approach gave Forest Service land managers greater discretionary authority to implement utilitarian forest management strategies, shifting the emphasis from commodity production toward a concept of ecosystem management and long-term sustainability.[232] This management philosophy maximized ecological, economic and social benefits, including outdoor recreation within the National Forest System. This spurred development of additional ski areas on national forest land, which made up one-third of all ski resorts opened in the United States during the 1960s. In Oregon, these included Anthony Lakes in the Wallow-Whitman National Forest in 1963, Mt. Ashland in the Siskiyou National Forest in 1964 and Mt. Hood Meadows in the Mount Hood National Forest in 1968.

The early 1970s marked a significant milestone transforming how the Forest Service managed national forest lands with the passage of the National Environmental Policy Act (NEPA). NEPA was the first major environmental law in the United States. It requires federal land management agencies to assess the environmental effects of proposed actions before making decisions on development. NEPA covers a broad range of activities, including how private-sector entities, including recreational services providers, operate under federal permit. NEPA also established a mechanism for the public to review proposals and participate in the decision-making process regarding development on public lands.

NEPA significantly changed how the Forest Service managed recreation within national forests, requiring analysis of the environmental impacts of proposed development projects, including ski resorts. Before NEPA, permitting ski resorts was generally less cumbersome, and projects were promptly approved. However, from the late 1960s onward, resort development proposals were often blocked by environmental challenges and experienced delays in permitting.[233] At the same time, environmental groups became more concerned about the effects of recreation on wildlife habitats, water quality and wilderness areas. Downhill skiing was a particular target due to the significant environmental impacts of ski area development.

As ski areas encountered challenges to their development plans, some operators blamed the Forest Service's permitting process for giving too much discretion to local authorities, making it difficult for resorts to overcome environmental opposition.[234] Others blamed an overly complicated permitting process that made it difficult for ski areas to grow organically and adopt new technologies and safety standards.

The National Forest Ski Area Permit Act (NFSAPA) of 1986 sought to resolve some of the concerns with permitting. Before the NFSAPA, resort developers had to apply for two separate permits for operation. The first permit covered infrastructure development for structures such as lodges and lifts, issued with a maximum term of thirty years. Ski trails and other land uses required a separate permit, issued annually. That process, described by resort operators as "cumbersome and confusing," made it challenging for ski resort operators to raise investment capital and manage long-range planning.[235]

The NFSAPA ended the dual-permitting system and established a forty-year term for permits without specific limits on acreage.[236] These changes were intended to streamline the process for applicants while facilitating planning and financing for resort operators. The NFSAPA also explicitly authorized Nordic and alpine skiing on suitable national forest land. However, it did not specifically clarify how ski areas might develop non-winter activities. The ambiguous wording limited how ski areas could develop off-season activities while leaving local Forest Service officials with significant discretion for approving projects on a case-by-case basis.[237]

The Ski Area Recreational Opportunity Enhancement Act of 2011 attempted to fix those problems by clarifying the guidelines for developing year-round recreational opportunities. The act envisioned summer activities such as zip lines, disc golf and mountain biking, recognizing that year-round recreation and associated facilities were essential to the long-term viability of ski areas. Notably, the legislation allowed resorts to propose the development of summertime recreational activities without requiring a separate permit.[238] However, the guidelines also limited certain activities such as water slides and amusement parks that would require high-impact infrastructure development on national forest land.

Over the last fifty years, outdoor recreation has become a significant source of economic growth for gateway communities adjacent to national forests. Today, 122 ski areas are located on national forest lands, comprising about 60 percent of the nation's downhill skiing capacity.[239] However, there is also growing public concern about the impact of these activities on the environment.[240]

This trend reflects a growing awareness of how recreational activities such as skiing, mountain biking and hiking contribute to environmental degradation, species endangerment and habitat destruction. NEPA and the permitting process have become the mechanism through which the Forest Service attempts to balance the increasing demand for recreational access with the environmental impacts of these activities.

THE SPECIAL USE PERMITTING PROCESS

Of the 473 ski areas operating in the United States, 122 are on national forest lands. These resorts occupy less than one-tenth of a percent of the entire National Forest System land base but account for around half of all annual skier visits nationwide.[241] According to the National Visitor Use Monitoring Program, around 16 percent of all visitors to the national forests cite downhill skiing and/or snowboarding as their primary activities.[242]

The Forest Service estimates that winter recreation contributes about $2.9 billion to local economies, supporting about 41,200 jobs nationwide. The number of jobs and the amount of economic activity generated by skiing on national forest lands is roughly equivalent to the revenue derived from forest products extracted from the National Forest System.[243]

When the Forest Service initially began allowing the development of ski areas on national forest lands, it employed a concessionaire model used by other public-private partnerships. Under this system, in use to this day, the Forest Service allows private investors to develop the infrastructure and manage operations on system lands. The ski areas, in turn, paid a user fee based on income derived from their commercial activities.

Fees go directly back to the federal treasury to help fund Forest Service activities and other programs. The fee amount is determined using a formula based on income generated from lift ticket sales, lessons and additional revenue. Rent payments vary on a scale from 1.5 up to 4 percent based on income levels. According to industry analysis, this works out to an average of around 2 percent of gross profits nationally.[244] In recent years, resorts operating on national forest lands generated approximately $37 million annually in revenue-based rent payments sent back to the government.[245]

Mt. Bachelor operates under a special-use permit administered by the Deschutes National Forest. A special-use authorization allows occupancy and use of, rights to or privileges on national forest land.[246] The Forest Service grants permission for specific land uses covering a fixed period. Permits are required whenever an entity intends to occupy, use or build on national forest land for personal or business purposes, whether the duration is temporary or long-term. A permit is required whenever an applicant charges a fee or derives income from the use of national forest land.

Around 80 percent of the Deschutes National Forest is considered available for winter recreation based on an average snow line of around five thousand feet, where conditions allow for adequate seasonal snow coverage for recreation. That area offers day use opportunities such as developed ski areas, groomed snowmobile areas and marked snowshoe trails, providing users with access and infrastructure supporting winter recreation activities.[247] Because the Forest Service lacks funding and personnel to operate winter recreation programs directly, it works with external stakeholders to provide these services to the public. This is done primarily by issuing special-use permits to outfitter-guides and resort operators.

Recreational proposals are evaluated based on social, environmental and economic/managerial factors. The social dimension concerns how visitor and community needs are being met in terms of visitor use and demand, how the public values the services being offered on public lands, health and safety, community stability, social acceptability and quality of life. The environmental dimension concerns protecting and conserving resources and natural settings for current and future generations. The managerial (or economic) dimension considers the potential impacts on the local community regarding jobs, economic development and tax revenues.

The Forest Service issues thousands of special-use permits to outfitters, guides and resort operators. The permit period may be as short as one day for events such as a concert or a bicycle race or up to forty years for users like ski resorts. In the case of ski areas, the Forest Service requires that resort operators prepare master development plans (MDPs) identifying an area's existing and desired conditions and the proposed improvements within the permit boundary.[248] The plan must cover physical infrastructure and operational components such as lifts and lodge facilities, locations for ski runs, snowmaking capabilities, slope-side amenities and non-skiing-related recreational opportunities.

Development plans help the ski areas articulate a long-range vision for how they will use public lands and assist the Forest Service in anticipating the impacts of future use. The plans also provide local governments, agencies and the public with information about how the proposal may affect them. Development plans serve a vital business function for resort operators, helping to raise capital and providing financial reporting for investors, shareholders and the government.

When issuing a permit for a ski area, the Forest Service will review a proposal and then accept, modify or deny the resort's development plan. These documents are intended to be dynamic and can be amended or revised periodically to reflect changing opportunities, market demands or agency administrative requirements.[249] Any proposed infrastructure improvements within the permit area must receive Forest Service approval before implementation.

The Forest Service reviews the conceptual projects contained in each plan to determine if they align with its goals and objectives. This is often a collaborative process whereby the Forest Service assists the resort operator in developing an acceptable proposal. In doing so, the Forest Service defines the scope of its environmental review based on the purposes and needs outlined in the plan.

The Forest Service must consider a variety of externalities when determining whether to approve a permit application. These include possible environmental damages, effects on wildlife, noise and air pollution, traffic and congestion, changes to the landscape and potential damage to archaeological sites and areas of unique cultural value.[250]

Acceptance of an MDP does not imply authorization to proceed with construction or implementation of any proposed projects. Some projects proposed in an MDP will require a more in-depth, site-specific evaluation as part of the Forest Service's environmental review and analysis. This review falls under the National Environmental Policy Act (NEPA), under direction provided by the National Forest Management Act.[251]

NEPA requires that agencies evaluate any potential impacts of proposed activities, including their effects on environmental, cultural and economic resources. Proposed projects must present alternative options so that decision-makers and the public can evaluate trade-offs of multiple plans, with options for mitigating potential impacts. The forest supervisor is responsible for analyzing and preparing environmental assessments or environmental impact statements relative to the site proposal.

In some cases, environmental impact statements (EIS) have presented obstacles for resort operators. Critics charge that the EIS process can be costly and time-consuming. Public comment periods and hearings often cause delays, requiring significant revisions or even leading to denial of proposed projects.[252] Environmental groups have used the EIS process to block development plans that negatively impact air and water quality or wildlife habitat.

Due to the increasing frequency of such challenges, ski areas attempt to tailor development plans to mitigate environmental degradation. This effort includes limiting road construction, designing lower-profile buildings and lifts, reducing sprawl and minimizing visual impacts on the landscape. Operators try to achieve sustainability by effectively managing water use, waste disposal and greenhouse gas emissions. Some resorts are also integrating development plans that minimize habitat fragmentation and help with wildfire mitigation.

Some stakeholders have criticized various aspects of this process. For example, skeptics charge that the government's approval process for resort development strongly favors the ski industry at the expense of noncorporate stakeholders and environmental interests. This critique asserts that the industry has excessive power to shape project proposals and form the alternative plans forwarded to the Forest Service for environmental assessment.[253] Additionally, resort operators can influence the environmental review by selecting an outside contractor to conduct the review and providing the information and technical expertise supporting the government's study.

Conversely, critics from the ski industry complain that environmental assessments often take years to complete and that the NEPA process makes it easy for special-interest groups to use the law to challenge development.[254] Another criticism is that the permitting process is often unpredictable due to variations in requirements among Forest Service administrative units. Ultimately, the nature of the permitting process makes it essential that resort operators engage closely with key stakeholders and the public through every stage of the process.

During its history, Mt. Bachelor's relationship with the Deschutes National Forest has been highly effective by industry standards. Its most recent MDP process included numerous pre-project meetings with citizens, environmental groups and key stakeholders before submitting a final plan to the Forest Service. After the Forest Service received comments from the public and provided responses, its Record of Decision was signed in early 2013 without public appeals.[255] Mt. Bachelor and Forest Service officials involved in the process considered it smooth and efficient by industry standards.[256]

CHAPTER 7

THE ATHLETES OF MOUNT BACHELOR

S ince Mt. Bachelor's establishment in 1958, the resort has become an incubator for athletic talent, turning Central Oregon into a premier training destination for elite athletes. That legacy began in the 1920s with the Skyliners and continues today through the Mt. Bachelor Sports Education Foundation (MBSEF).

From its origin in the 1920s, the Skyliners club embraced a tradition of outdoor sports education and competition. The club's original mission was "to promote all forms of outdoor recreation, especially hiking, camping, mountain climbing, skiing, snowshoeing, [and] skating."[257]

During the late 1920s, Skyliners members competed in regional races, such as the famous Fort Klamath to Crater Lake ski race started in 1927 by the Crater Lake Ski Club. That event was a forty-two-mile round-trip cross-county race stretching from Fort Klamath to Crater Lake, with an elevation gain of nearly three thousand feet.[258] The race offered cash prizes and drew top skiers from the Pacific Northwest and California.

Manfred Jacobson of McCloud, California, won the inaugural event in 1927 and won again in 1928, the first year that the club awarded the Klamath Cup, a silver trophy worth $1,600. According to the event rules, whoever won the race twice would retire the trophy. Bend's Emil Nordeen won the 1929 race, and Jacobson took it back in 1930; therefore, whoever won the 1931 race would earn the right to retire the trophy.

Nordeen won the 1931 event in a highly anticipated race, setting a record time of five hours and thirty-five minutes and winning by a wide margin

Emil Nordeen holding the Klamath Cup after his 1931 victory in the Fort Klamath to Crater Lake ski race. *Deschutes County Historical Society.*

over Jacobson. The Crater Lake Ski Club offered Nordeen the Klamath Cup for his victory. In 1960, Nordeen bequeathed the trophy to the Swedish Ski Federation, and it now sits in the Skidlöparmuseum in Norsjö, Sweden.

In 1930, the Skyliners hosted its first "snow carnival" at the McKenzie Pass ski hill, providing an opportunity to showcase Central Oregon's top athletes. The event included ski jumping and a twenty-five-mile cross-country race drawing some of the best skiers from the Pacific Northwest. Nordeen and Nels Skjersaa placed first and third in a highly competitive field.[259] Skjersaa earned a spot on the All-American Cross-Country Ski Team the next season. The following year, the Skyliners joined the Pacific Northwest Ski Association and continued sending athletes to compete against the top clubs from around the region.

In 1936, when the club moved to its new location above Tumalo Creek, the facilities were built with competition in mind. With the help of the Civilian Conservation Corps, the club constructed ski jumps, cross-country trails and a slalom course. The first event at the new facility was held in 1938, showcasing a new generation of Central Oregon skiing talent. One of Bend's top skiers, Olaf Skjersaa, made the first official jump from the new ski hill during that competition.[260]

The club held its first race on Bachelor Butte in June 1941. The course started on the summit, descending 2,500 feet to the timberline. Olaf Skjersaa won the race, completing the one-mile course in just over one minute.[261] Organized winter competition paused during World War II but resumed in the fall of 1947. During the mid-1950s, an effort was made to refurbish the old Skyliners ski hill above Tumalo Creek with new rope tows, an alpine racecourse and a competition ski jump.

When Bachelor Butte opened, the Skyliners club decided to stop operating the ski hill above Tumalo Creek and focus its efforts on promoting outdoor activities and sports education.[262] The area continued to be used for occasional competitions until the mid-1960s; however, most of the Skyliners' training and events moved to the new ski area on Bachelor Butte.

Shortly after Mt. Bachelor opened, the resort began hosting club, high school and college ski competitions. It was soon attracting elite-level skiers for training and competition. In August 1963, Bob Beattie, coach of the U.S. Olympic Ski Team, brought a group of his athletes to Mt. Bachelor for a summer training camp in preparation for the 1964 games in Innsbruck, Austria. The team stayed in cabins at Elk Lake and accessed the late-summer snowfields using a portable rope tow.[263] The training group included Jean Saubert, who regularly trained at Mt. Bachelor and went on to win a bronze medal in the slalom and a silver medal in the giant slalom at the Innsbruck games.

In 1965, Mt. Bachelor hosted the Junior National Ski Championships, a four-way event including alpine slalom, giant slalom, cross-country and jumping. The jumping event was held on the northwest slope of Pilot Butte in Bend using a temporary jump and snow trucked in from a higher elevation.[264] The championship drew over 2,500 competitors and spectators and raised Central Oregon's profile as a venue for elite-level competition.

The new ski hill at Mt. Bachelor offered the Skyliners a significantly improved area for training and competition; however, the club still lacked a professional coaching staff. In the early 1960s, there was an effort to bring over an Austrian coach to run the alpine racing program, but the club couldn't raise funds to hire a full-time coach.[265] Instead, the Skyliners recruited Frank Cammack to run the alpine training program part-time starting in 1962.

Cammack had learned to ski around his family's ranch near Wenatchee, Washington, and was introduced to ski jumping at the Leavenworth Winter Sports Club. He eventually became a top Nordic combined skier for the University of Idaho, helping his team win three consecutive Northwest Intercollegiate Ski Championship titles. In 1957, Cammack won the Nordic combined at the U.S. Skiing Championships, earning him a spot on the U.S. team at the World Championships in Finland. Cammack was selected for the 1960 Olympic team but didn't compete after suffering a severe injury in a logging accident in Idaho.

Cammack briefly coached the Cascade Ski Club at the Multorpor ski area on Mount Hood while living in Portland but moved with his wife to Bend in 1962 after taking a job at the Brooks-Scanlon mill. A week after arriving in Bend, Cammack attended a Skyliners meeting and was recruited to run the club's alpine program. He started with fourteen skiers but doubled that number within a few years.

Above: U.S. Olympic team summer training camp above the Pine Marten knob, September 1964. *Deschutes County Historical Society.*

Left: Frank Cammack, Skyliners ski coach from 1962–72. *Courtesy of Mt. Bachelor Sports Education Foundation.*

Cliff Blann, Mt. Bachelor's operations manager, had two children skiing under Cammack and ensured that the team always had space for training. However, during the early years of the program, funding was limited. Cammack recalled taking his athletes down to the Deschutes River to collect sticks for slalom gates and boot-packing the training area before each practice. Despite the austere training conditions, Cammack developed numerous world-class skiers during his time as head coach from 1962 to 1972, including Olympians Kiki Cutter and Mike Lafferty. After leaving as head coach, Cammack remained closely involved with Skyliners and later served on the Mt. Bachelor Sports Education Foundation board.

Mt. Bachelor entered the spotlight as a racing venue in March 1972 when it hosted the U.S. national championships for giant slalom and slalom, the most prestigious event held at the resort up to that time. The event drew the top North American skiers to a giant slalom course set on the Thunderbird run and a slalom course on Tippy Toe.[266] The field included former Skyliners member Mike Lafferty, who had finished fourteenth in the downhill just a few months before at the 1972 Olympics in Sapporo, Japan.[267]

During the mid-1970s, the Skyliners had challenges maintaining a professional coaching staff on a limited budget. Consequently, the club turned over its coaching duties to the resort's ski school; however, that arrangement didn't last. In 1986, the board decided that it would be best to transition the Skyliners into a tax-exempt nonprofit foundation to improve its financial standing. This involved changing its name to the Mt. Bachelor Ski Education Foundation, later known as the Mt. Bachelor Sports Education Foundation (MBSEF). Over the years, the alpine training program expanded to other disciplines, including cross-county, freeride skiing and snowboarding.

Dennis Oliphant served as the first director of MBSEF's Nordic training program in the early 1980s.[268] As the Nordic network expanded, it attracted top-caliber skiers drawn by the demanding trails and a long spring training season. By the 1990s, the Nordic Center had hosted several major race events, including the 1994 North American Championships, the 1995 U.S. National Junior Nordic Championships and the 1996 U.S. National Championships. Numerous Olympic athletes trained locally at Mt. Bachelor, including Dan Simoneau, Mike Devecka, Leslie Bancroft-Krichko, Suzanne King, Ben Husaby and Justin Wadsworth.

Mt. Bachelor was also a training ground for the winter biathlon at various times during its history. Olympic biathlete Jay Bowerman came to Bend in the summer of 1968 and began training around the old Skyliners ski hill and Mount Bachelor. There were no regularly groomed cross-country trails in the area, so Bowerman borrowed a snowmobile owned by Jack Meissner to set tracks for training. He and Meissner's son Ernie practiced shooting using impromptu ranges set up on national forest land to the east of Mount Bachelor.[269]

During the 1980s, MBSEF tried to develop a biathlon training program, led by 1988 Olympic team member Rich Gross and using a range on a gravel pit area near the edge of the Nordic network.[270] The athletes had to set up the range before each practice because the Forest Service didn't allow a permanent training site within the special-use permit area. Gross ran the training program until the early 1990s, but the shooting facilities proved difficult to maintain. The range eventually became inactive, and MBSEF dropped its biathlon program.

As snowboarding became an Olympic sport for the 1998 games in Nagano, Japan, MBSEF expanded its training program to include snowboard racing and freeride. Mt. Bachelor jumped into the spotlight in 1998 when it hosted the FIS Snowboard World Cup and U.S. Snowboard Grand Prix, events that helped select the U.S. Olympic teams for giant slalom and half-pipe. Bend native Chris Klug earned his Olympic berth in the giant slalom at the event.[271] Mt. Bachelor again hosted a Grand Prix and Olympic qualifying event in early 2002 for the games in Salt Lake City.

The MBSEF program evolved with the sport and eventually included training for slopestyle, half-pipe, gates and all-mountain freeriding skills. Snowboard cross was held for the first time as an Olympic event during the 2006 games in Torino, Italy, and slopestyle was added for the 2014 games in Sochi, Russia. The MBSEF program produced numerous word-class snowboarders, including Chris Klug, Adam Smith, Kent Callister, Ben Ferguson and Sean FitzSimons.

Since the resort opened, Mt. Bachelor and MBSEF have hosted numerous iconic competitions. The oldest is the Sun Cup, part of the Pacific Northwest Ski Association's Northwest Cup Series and a qualifying race for Junior Nationals. The race initially began as a Skyliners event in the mid-1960s and included a downhill course staged on the Cliffhanger run. The event drew top junior skiers from the Pacific Northwest, including many of Mt. Bachelor's elite athletes such as Kevin Francis, Tommy Ford and Eric Holmer.

Since 2003, MBSEF has sponsored the Great Nordeen cross-country race, named after Bend's iconic racer Emil Nordeen. The modern Nordeen is a point-to-point race beginning at Mt. Bachelor and following Forest Service roads over thirty kilometers to Wanoga Sno-Park.

MBSEF also runs the Pole Pedal Paddle (PPP), Bend's signature multisport event. The inaugural race was held in 1976 and founded by Jenny Sheldon, a ski coach for the Skyliners who modeled the event after a similar race held in Jackson Hole. Initially, the race consisted of a three-mile cross-country ski leg at Dutchman Flat, an eighteen-mile bike ride down Century Drive and a one-mile run around Drake Park, finishing with a paddle leg up and down Mirror Pond. The first race drew only twelve teams and sixteen individual competitors.

Today, thousands of racers participate in the annual event. The modern course starts with a short downhill ski adjacent to Mt. Bachelor's Red Chair, followed by an eight-kilometer Nordic race and a twenty-two-mile bike ride down to Bend. After the bike leg, racers transition into a five-mile trail run, followed by a mile-and-a-half paddle on the Deschutes River and then a half-mile sprint to the finish line.

The MBSEF continues the Skyliners' legacy by supporting winter sports programs for hundreds of junior athletes competing in alpine and Nordic skiing, snowboarding and freeride events. In 2020, it opened a state-of-the-art training center with weight and fitness areas, a ski wax room and a trampoline facility where freeride skiers and snowboarders can train for aerial maneuvers. The training center is named in honor of Bill Healy and features a permanent museum exhibit on Healy and Mt. Bachelor's history.

MT. BACHELOR OLYMPIAN PROFILES

Alpine Skiing and Snowboarding

GENE GILLIS was born in 1925 in Bend, Oregon. His father, Jere Gillis, was a member and president of the Skyliners ski club during the early 1930s. The younger Gillis began skiing at the age of three. At Bend High School, he was a talented multisport athlete, excelling at football, basketball, track and field, tennis, golf and skiing. Gillis played football at the University of Oregon before joining the marines in 1945. After World War II, Gillis was named to the 1948 U.S. Alpine Olympic Ski Team competing in St. Moritz, Switzerland, but did not race after sustaining an injury during training. After the Olympics, Gillis coached local junior skiers in Bend and was a central figure in the early development of the Mt. Bachelor ski area. Later in his career, Gillis was involved in developing other ski areas, including Stratton Mountain Resort in Vermont and Keystone Resort in Colorado.

JEAN SAUBERT was born in 1942 in Roseburg, Oregon, and raised in the town of Cascadia. She graduated from Lakeview High School in 1960 and learned to ski at Warner Canyon and Hoodoo ski areas. During her college years at Oregon State, she trained and raced competitively at Mount Hood and Mt. Bachelor. Saubert made the U.S. Ski Team in 1962 and competed in the World Championships in Chamonix, France, where she finished sixth in the giant slalom. In 1963 and 1964, she was the U.S. downhill and giant slalom champion and won the

Jean Saubert with French skier Marielle Goitschel at the 1964 Winter Olympic Games in Innsbruck, Austria. *AP.*

slalom and combined championships in 1964. At the 1964 Winter Olympics in Innsbruck, Saubert won a bronze medal in slalom and a silver in the giant slalom. During her racing career, Saubert won a total of eight U.S. championships. She was inducted into the National Ski Hall of Fame in 1976 and was a torchbearer for the 2002 Winter Olympics in Salt Lake City, Utah.

MICHAEL LAFFERTY was born in 1948 in Eugene, Oregon. Michael's father, Paul, was the first officer to join the Tenth Mountain Division at Fort Lewis during World War II and later served as a ski coach for the University of Oregon. The younger Lafferty learned to ski at Willamette Pass and raced as a junior skier for the Skyliners club at Mt. Bachelor. After graduating

Michael Lafferty, 1972 Olympian in the downhill. *Courtesy of Mt. Bachelor Sports Education Foundation.*

from South Eugene High School in 1966, Lafferty raced for the University of Colorado in Boulder. He earned his first top ten World Cup result in 1969 in the downhill at Val-d'Isère, France. Lafferty was on the U.S. Winter Olympic team in 1972, where he finished fourteenth in the downhill in Sapporo, Japan. In 1974, Lafferty finished third in the World Cup downhill season standings, the best finish ever by an American male.

CHRISTINA "KIKI" CUTTER was born in 1949 in Bend, Oregon, and learned to ski with the Skyliners junior race program under coach Frank Cammack. She developed early as a racer and was invited to train with the U.S. team at age fifteen. At seventeen, she won the U.S. Junior Downhill Championship in 1967. The following year, she earned a late spot on the 1968 U.S. Olympic team competing in Grenoble, France. Cutter was the only American woman at the games to ski in all three alpine disciplines: slalom, giant slalom and downhill. After the Olympics, Cutter was the first American skier to win a World Cup title in the slalom event at Kirkerudbakken, Norway. Cutter won her fifth and final World Cup race at St. Gervais, France, in 1970. Cutter had five World Cup victories during her career before retiring from international racing at twenty. Cutter was elected to the U.S. National Ski Hall of Fame in 1993.

Christina "Kiki" Cutter, the first American skier to win a World Cup title. *Courtesy of Colorado Snowsports Museum and Hall of Fame.*

CHRIS KLUG was born in 1972 in Vail, Colorado. When he was four, his family moved to Bend, where he began snowboarding at Mt. Bachelor. Klug was the U.S. amateur slalom and super-G snowboarding champion in 1989 and began competing as a professional snowboarder while still a student at Mountain View High School. Klug eventually won four World Cup races, three Grand Prix titles and five U.S. titles. In 1991, Klug was diagnosed with primary sclerosing cholangitis and received a liver transplant in 2000. Shortly after the surgery, he returned to training and qualified for the 2002 games in Salt Lake City, Utah. He won a bronze medal in the parallel giant slalom and is the only organ transplant recipient to win a medal in any Olympics. He has since become a vocal advocate for organ donation. Klug finished sixth at the 1998 games in Nagano, Japan, and qualified for his third Olympic team in 2010 in Vancouver, Canada.

LAURENNE ROSS was born in 1988 in Alberta, Canada, and started skiing at the age of two at the Snow Valley Ski Club outside Edmonton. When she was five, her family moved to Klamath Falls, Oregon, and she began training with MBSEF two years later. She was selected for the U.S. Ski Team at age seventeen in 2006. Ross made her World Cup debut in 2010 and finished tenth at the 2011 World Championships. She earned her first of two World Cup podiums in 2013 by placing second in the downhill at Garmisch-Partenkirchen, Germany. Ross made her first Olympic appearance in 2014 in Sochi, Russia, placing eleventh overall downhill. In 2018, she competed in the games at Pyeongchang, South Korea, finishing fifteenth in the super-G and downhill events. During her career, Ross achieved twenty-six top ten World Cup results. Ross's grandfather, Allan Purvis, was an Olympic gold medalist and former captain of Canada's 1952 Olympic ice hockey team. Ross is a graduate of Klamath Union High School and the University of Oregon.

Tommy Ford was born in 1989 in Hanover, New Hampshire, and raised in Bend. He began his skiing career on Mt. Bachelor at the age of two. Ford trained with MBSEF as a youth racer and joined the U.S. Ski Team at age twenty. During his career, Ford represented the United States in three winter Olympics and four world championships. At the 2010 Winter Olympics in Vancouver, British Columbia, Ford finished twenty-sixth in the giant slalom, and at the 2018 games in Pyeongchang, South Korea, he finished twentieth. Ford's first World Cup top ten finish came in 2017 for the giant slalom. In 2019, Ford won the Birds of Prey giant slalom at Beaver Creek, Colorado, capturing his first career victory on the World Cup tour and becoming one of only four Americans ever to win a world cup giant slalom race. During that season, he finished fifth in the world in giant slalom rankings and earned three podium finishes at World Cup giant slalom races. His 2021 season ended early following a crash at a race in Switzerland. After not racing for over a year, Ford was selected for the 2022 U.S. Olympic team as a discretionary pick and went on to a twelfth-place finish in giant slalom at the games in Beijing, China, his best finish in three Olympics.

Kent Callister was born in 1995 in San Diego and lived for a time in Australia. He moved to Bend with his family at the age of nine and is a graduate of Summit High School. After arriving in Bend, Callister transitioned from skateboarding to snowboarding, specializing in the half-pipe. Although Callister trained at Mt. Bachelor with MBSEF, he competed internationally for Australia and was selected for the U.S. and Australian half-pipe teams during the 2012–13 season. At his first World Championship in 2013, he placed fifteenth, and he finished ninth at the 2014 Olympic games in Sochi, Russia. In 2015, Callister achieved his first World Cup podium in Park City, Utah, winning bronze, and later that year, he placed sixth at the

World Championships in Kreischberg, Austria. At the 2018 Olympic Games in Pyeongchang, South Korea, Callister finished tenth overall.

BEN FERGUSON was born in 1995 in Boise, Idaho, and began snowboarding at Mt. Bachelor at the age of six with MBSEF. At age ten, he competed in the United States Snowboard and Freeski Association (USASA) Nationals, winning slopestyle and finishing second in the half-pipe. In 2012, Ferguson competed in the inaugural Youth Olympic Games in Innsbruck, Austria, winning the half-pipe contest and placing second in slopestyle. The following year, Ferguson qualified for the U.S. snowboard half-pipe team. Ferguson missed qualifying for the 2014 Games by one spot and then came back to qualify for the 2018 games in Pyeongchang, South Korea, in which he finished fourth. In 2016, Ferguson graduated from Mountain View High School in Bend. His younger brother, Gabe, is also a member of the U.S. snowboarding team.

SEAN FITZSIMONS was born in 2000 and grew up in Hood River, Oregon, graduating from Hood River Valley High School. He learned snowboarding on Mount Hood and later trained at Mt. Bachelor with the MBSEF snowboard team. FitzSimons competed professionally in three snowboard events: slopestyle, big air and half-pipe. He had his first World Cup win just three weeks before the 2022 Olympic Games in Beijing. FitzSimons competed in both slopestyle and big air events at the games, placing twelfth in slopestyle.

NORDIC AND BIATHLON

JAY BOWERMAN was born in 1942 in Seattle, Washington, the son of Bill Bowerman, the legendary track coach at the University of Oregon and cofounder of Nike. Bowerman attended North Eugene High School and graduated from the University of Oregon in 1966, where he was a member of the Reserve Officers' Training Corps (ROTC). After graduation, Bowerman served on active duty as an army officer in Anchorage, Alaska, where he trained with the army's winter biathlon team (cross-country skiing and rifle shooting). Bowerman moved to Bend after being named an alternate on the U.S. Olympic team for the 1968 games in Grenoble, France. In Bend, he continued training, often alone, around the old Skyliners ski hill and Mount Bachelor. During the winters, he used a snowmobile owned by Jack Meissner to set tracks for training and built impromptu ranges on the east side of Mount Bachelor to practice shooting. In 1969, Bowerman was the

U.S. national biathlon champion. At the 1972 Olympic Games in Sapporo, Japan, he finished forty-second individually and in sixth place on the men's relay team. Bowerman later taught high school biology in Bend and played an important role in the early development of the High Desert Museum and as the executive director of the Sunriver Nature Center.

MIKE DEVECKA was born in 1947 in Portland, Oregon, where his father managed the Multorpor Ski Area on Mount Hood. He began skiing at age five and ski jumping at eight. When he was fourteen, Devecka borrowed a pair of cross-country boots and skis to compete in the 1962 junior nationals in Steamboat, Colorado. Devecka did most of his early training at Mount Hood and later skied for Fort Lewis College, earning NCAA All American honors in 1968 and 1969, and was a member of the U.S. Ski Team during his college career. After serving in the army, Devecka moved to Bend in 1972. During his career, Devecka competed in both ski jumping and Nordic combined and was a four-time U.S. Olympic team member: in 1968, 1972, 1976 and 1980. He was the U.S. champion in the Nordic combined in 1972, 1974, 1975 and 1979; the 1974 national champion in the thirty-kilometer cross-country race; and the 1978 national champion in the ninety-meter jumping event. He is the only U.S. skier to win national championships in all three Nordic disciplines: jumping, cross-country and Nordic combined.

RICH GROSS was born in 1954 in Boise, Idaho. His early athletic career was as a cross-country runner and Alpine ski racer for Boise State College, and he didn't begin actively training for Nordic races until moving to Portland in the early 1980s. Gross eventually took up biathlon at the age of twenty-five after moving to Bend and meeting former Olympian Jay Bowerman, who taught Gross how to shoot and encouraged him to begin training for biathlon. After only a few years of training, primarily alone, Gross qualified for the 1984 Olympic Trials. After the trials, he returned to Bend and continued training with Bowerman's help and was named to the U.S. National Team before the 1988 Olympic trials. Gross qualified for the seven-man U.S. squad for the 1988 games in Calgary, Canada. However,

Rich Gross, 1988 Olympic biathlon team member who trained around Mount Bachelor with former Olympian Jay Bowerman. *Photograph by Bob Woodward.*

after becoming ill during the pre-Olympic competition in Europe, Gross attended but did not race at the games. After the Olympics, he continued to train at Mt. Bachelor's Nordic Center and qualified for the 1992 Olympic trials at the age of thirty-eight.

DAN SIMONEAU was born in 1959 in Farmington, Maine, and first came to Oregon in the 1970s to train for the Nordic World Championships. He was on the U.S. Ski Team from 1976 to 1988 and competed in the 1982, 1985 and 1987 world championships. Simoneau qualified for the 1980 winter games in Lake Placid as an alternate and then competed in the 1984 and 1988 Olympics. At the 1984 games in Sarajevo, he finished eighth in the 4x10-kilometer relay and eighteenth in the 15-kilometer event. Simoneau was second in a 30-kilometer event in Sweden in 1982 and was the U.S. champion in the 30-kilometer in 1987 and 1988. Simoneau returned to Central Oregon in 2003 and became the Nordic ski director for MBSEF in 2008. Simoneau has developed over a dozen local skiers who participated in the U.S. nationals and was recognized as "coach of the year" four times by the Pacific Northwest Ski Association. Simoneau is a 1986 graduate of the University of Oregon and a three-time individual winner of the Pole Pedal Paddle, Bend's premier multisport race.

LESLIE BANCROFT-KRICHKO was born in 1959 and grew up in Paris, Maine. She began her athletic career as a runner but transitioned to cross-country skiing when her high school started a team. Soon after, Krichko won the Maine state championship as a sophomore and then made the U.S. junior national team, winning several races during her senior year in high school. She was invited to train with the U.S. national team and earned a spot on the 1980 team competing in Lake Placid, New York. Krichko finished thirty-third in the 5-kilometer race and twenty-eighth in the 10-kilometer and placed seventh in a relay event. Krichko could not compete in the 1984 Olympics due to a foot injury. After retiring from racing, she moved to Oregon to attend Portland State University and later returned to skiing. Krichko placed fifth at the 1985 nationals in Oregon and qualified for the 1988 games in

Two-time Olympian Leslie Bancroft-Krichko, who returned from retirement to make the 1988 games in Calgary, Canada. *Photograph by Bob Woodward.*

Calgary, Canada, where she placed thirty-first in the 5-kilometer race, thirty-sixth in the 10-kilometer event and eighth in the 4x5-kilometer relay.

Suzanne King was born in 1964 in New Haven, Connecticut. At the 1988 winter games in Nagano, Japan, King finished fourteenth in the 15-kilometer, forty-third in the 30-kilometer freestyle and fifteenth in the 4x5-kilometer relay. In the 1994 Olympics in Lillehammer, Norway, she was fifty-first in the 30-kilometer classic. She also competed at the 1997 World Championships in Trondheim, Norway. King stopped racing the following year but returned to ski marathon races in 2003. She was a five-time women's champion of the Pole Pedal Paddle and held the record for the most consecutive victories by a female racer. For many years, she taught Spanish and French at Bend's High Desert Middle School.

Ben Husaby was born in 1965 in Eden Prairie, Minnesota, and named to the U.S. Ski Team junior squad in 1985. He raced for the University of Colorado in cross-country running and Nordic skiing. Husaby competed at the 1991 World Winter University Games, where he placed fifteenth in the fifteen-kilometer. After moving to Bend, Husaby qualified for the 1992 winter games in Albertville, France, finishing twenty-sixth in the ten-kilometer event. He qualified again for the 1994 Olympic Games in Lillehammer, Norway, finishing fifty-second in the ten-kilometer event and fifty-third in the fifty-kilometer. During his career, Husaby was an eleven-time National Champion in Nordic skiing at the junior, senior and master levels. He later became a full-time ski coach and served as the MBSEF Nordic director. Husaby was the six-time individual men's champion of the Pole Pedal Paddle.

Justin Wadsworth was born in 1968 in La Jolla, California. At twelve, he began cross-country skiing and competed with the U.S. junior rowing team before focusing on ski racing. Wadsworth was a four-time U.S. champion and three-time Olympian in 1994 at Lillehammer, Norway; in 1998 in Nagano, Japan; and in 2002 in Salt Lake City. At the 2002 games, he was a member of the fifth place 4x10-kilometer relay. Wadsworth was named head coach of the Canadian cross-country ski team in 2010 and led the team at the 2014 Winter Olympic Games in Sochi, Russia. In 2019, he was named head coach of Canada's Olympic biathlon team. Wadsworth was an eight-time individual men's champion of the Pole Pedal Paddle, holding the record for most individual victories in the history of the race.

CHAPTER 8

LOOKING TO THE FUTURE

F or generations, Mount Bachelor and the surrounding forests have played an important role in Central Oregon's cultural and economic history. In developing the ski area on Bachelor Butte, Bill Healy and other visionaries understood the mountain's potential to transform a struggling logging town into a hub for outdoor recreation and tourism. Healy's timing was auspicious, coming at the start of the boom period for American skiing.

Today, Central Oregon's tourism industry contributes as much as $960 million to the local economy, with around 70 percent of visitors coming for outdoor recreation, primarily within the Deschutes National Forest.[272] This amounts to approximately 4.5 million visitors each year, supporting nearly 10,000 workers employed by the tourism industry.[273]

Over the last two decades, Central Oregon has been among the fastest-growing regions in the state and Bend one of the most dynamic small cities in the country. The influx of new residents has helped diversify the economy away from its dependence on tourism, bringing in new jobs and development. However, the region's phenomenal success has not come without negative aspects. Rapid growth has exacerbated a housing crisis, increased traffic on the roads and damaged popular recreational sites because of crowding and overuse.

Forest Service data shows that recreational visits to the Deschutes National Forest roughly doubled between 2013 and 2018. Visits to popular areas like the Three Sisters Wilderness increased even more, with some trailheads seeing spikes in usage between 300 and 500 percent. According to the Central Cascades Wilderness Strategies Project, overuse has damaged vulnerable ecosystems through crowding, human and dog waste, trail bed expansion and the introduction of invasive species.[274] These challenges recently led the Forest Service to limit day-use entry at some of the most popular trailheads accessing the Mount Jefferson, Mount Washington and Three Sisters Wilderness areas.

The region faces another potentially disruptive threat due to climate change. The most recent Oregon Climate Assessment painted an ominous picture of the observed and projected effects in the area.[275] Since 1895, Oregon's annual average temperature has increased by about 2.2°F per century. The six warmest years on record have all occurred since 2012, according to the National Oceanic and Atmospheric Administration's Centers for Environmental Information. Given current trends for greenhouse gas emissions, temperatures are projected to increase on average by 5°F by 2050 and 8.2°F by 2080.

These changes will significantly affect the amount of annual precipitation in Oregon and how much of it falls as snow during wintertime. Since 1950, Oregon's spring snowpack has decreased at nearly every snow-observing

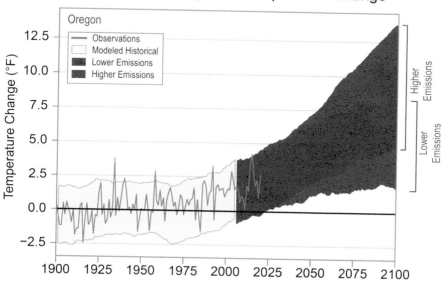

Observed and projected changes in near-surface air temperature for Oregon as of 2022. *Figure used with permission of NOAA National Centers for Environmental Information.*

station across the state. Some of the most significant declines have been observed east of the central Cascade Range in the Deschutes National Forest.

Since the mid-1900s, snowpack levels in the Cascades have declined about 60 percent due to more precipitation falling as rain than as snow.[276] This trend has year-round implications because of the critical role of the winter snowpack in storing water supply for release during the spring and summer months when there is little precipitation east of the Cascades. By 2080, winter snow cover is expected to decrease by seven to eight weeks at many locations in the Cascades, with minimal snow remaining by early April. Climate change effects are also evident in the rapid disappearance of the region's glaciers. Snow surveys from the 1950s identified around thirty glaciers in the Central Oregon Cascades. Today, only thirteen remain, and several of these are at risk of vanishing soon.[277]

Warmer temperatures and declining winter snowpack also impact streamflow, potentially threatening the economically important summer recreation industry.[278] According to recent projections, early snowmelt in the south-central Cascades will result in summertime streamflow losses of 40 to 60 percent by 2040 and as much as 80 percent by 2080. This means that rivers across Oregon may see their highest flow rates occurring earlier in the season and much lower flows in late summer.[279]

Gradual seasonal snowmelt is critical for providing adequate water for agricultural, municipal and public uses, including power production and recreation. Earlier snowmelts mean less instream flow during late summer when demand is higher. Earlier peak streamflow levels can also worsen erosion, degrade water quality and threaten sensitive aquatic habitats. Furthermore, thinning snowpack is expected to exacerbate the frequency and severity of droughts, potentially worsening the region's vulnerability to dangerous wildfires.

According to a recent Forest Service report, climate change will negatively affect snow-based winter activities across Central Oregon. However, effects at the local level will vary based on location and elevation.[280] Warmer temperatures will reduce the proportion of annual precipitation arriving as snow, while the rain-snow transition zone will move to higher elevations. One recent study estimated the costs to snowpack-dependent industries in Oregon could be as much as $4.2 billion by 2060, assuming current warming trends continue.[281]

These challenges come as the ski industry is experiencing slow growth and consolidation. Since the late 1980s, the number of ski resorts in the United States has declined from around 620 to approximately 460 today.

At the same time, winter sports participation in the United States over the last two decades has been largely stagnant.[282] Meanwhile, many resorts are experiencing shortened, more variable ski seasons and less reliable natural snow.[283] Later opening dates significantly impact resort profitability, often affecting operations during the critical early-winter holiday periods.

Several factors make Central Oregon's winter recreation particularly vulnerable to climate change. Some regional resorts have lower base areas, such as Willamette Pass (5,128 feet) and Hoodoo (4,668 feet). Both ski areas have struggled in recent years due to a lack of snow in the early season. To some degree, Mt. Bachelor is more resilient, with its higher base elevation of 6,300 feet. Nevertheless, the winter recreation economy tends to be highly sensitive to variations in temperature, snow levels and the timing of precipitation.[284]

Of all fifty states, Oregon has some of the greatest variation in skier visits between high and low snowfall years, according to data from the National Ski Areas Association (NSAA).[285] Lower-elevation ski areas and warmer average temperatures in the Pacific Northwest often mean more variability in conditions. Ski areas in the Pacific Northwest also tend to have less snowmaking capabilities than ski areas in other regions, leaving them less able to adapt to low-snow years.

Climate change is already having a measurable impact on winter recreation across Oregon, with effects expected to worsen in the future. A recent study in the *Journal of Global Environmental Change* estimated that Mt. Bachelor's ski season could drop from 180 to 68 days by 2090, while Hoodoo's season might disappear entirely.[286] The situation could be even worse for the lower-elevation cross-country ski areas and winter recreation sites. While Mt. Bachelor's Nordic Center sits at a relatively high 6,350 feet, the Virginia Meissner Sno-Park is around 1,000 feet lower and experiences more variable snow coverage.

Many ski areas, including Mt. Bachelor, are working to mitigate and adapt to these challenges. Unfortunately, skiing is an inherently carbon-intensive activity because most participants rely on air and ground transportation to access recreational sites. Most of Oregon's annual skier visits are considered day visits, with skiers traveling to and from home in a single trip rather than staying overnight near a ski area. Most of these visitors travel by car, with an average one-way trip of approximately seventy miles.[287]

Given this profile, Oregon ski resorts have few easy options to reduce the carbon footprint of guests traveling to the mountains. However, many

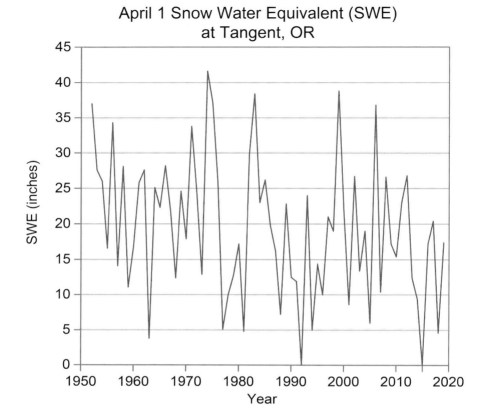

Variations in the annual snow water equivalent at the Tangent snow telemetry station, near the Virginia Meissner Sno-Park. *Figure used with permission of NOAA National Centers for Environmental Information.*

areas are taking steps to reduce emissions and achieve more sustainable operations. As part of this effort, Mt. Bachelor joined the Sustainable Slopes program, an environmental charter developed by the NSAA to address the impact of climate change on the winter recreation industry. The voluntary program helps resorts set goals for carbon reduction while offering funding to support sustainability projects at NSAA member ski areas.

In its most recent annual report, Mt. Bachelor committed to reducing its energy emissions by 50 percent, with a 75 percent waste diversion rate by 2030 compared with 2018 baseline standards. The resort has also pursued sustainability initiatives such as installing a solar panel array on the Nordic Lodge, using more LED lighting and building a biomass furnace to replace approximately 150,000 gallons of annual propane use and thus reduce the resort's overall emissions. While these efforts can make a difference at the margins, Mt. Bachelor—and the ski industry in general—will need to embrace significant adaptations to deal with the realities of shorter, more unpredictable winters.

MOUNT BACHELOR'S ROLE IN SCIENTIFIC RESEARCH

Sitting atop Mount Bachelor's 9,065-foot summit is the Mount Bachelor Observatory (MBO). This high-altitude atmospheric research station measures air pollution and the long-range transport of chemicals such as ozone, carbon monoxide, aerosols and mercury.[288] Professor Dan Jaffe at the University of Washington Bothell leads the research group and selected Mount Bachelor as the site for the research station.

Several factors make Mount Bachelor an ideal site for this observatory. Considerations included finding a high-elevation summit isolated from other mountains. It was also important to have electrical power, space for instrumentation and year-round access for researchers. Another significant advantage of Mount Bachelor's summit is that it allows researchers to collect air samples from the free troposphere.

The troposphere is the lowest layer of the atmosphere where most weather and climate processes occur. It is also where greenhouse gases, water vapor and clouds are transported. Therefore, it is an essential layer for studying climatic phenomena and tracking the long-range movement of air pollutants. Downslope winds bring air from this atmospheric layer down to Mount Bachelor's summit at night, which the observatory's sensors can sample.

The MBO is the only high-elevation tropospheric research site on the West Coast of the United States. It has continuously collected air samples since its establishment in 2004. MBO researchers have studied phenomena such as air pollutants transported from Asia and smoke plumes from western wildfires. Recent research conducted at the observatory has shown that particulates from wildfire smoke remain in the atmosphere longer than previously understood and can change weather patterns by scattering or absorbing solar radiation.[289]

Dr. Jaffe's group has published numerous papers in peer-reviewed scientific journals and collaborated with academic institutions, scientific nonprofits and research centers worldwide. The observatory receives funding from the

Summit lift terminal housing the equipment and workspace of the Mount Bachelor Observatory. *Photograph courtesy of Dan Jaffe.*

National Science Foundation and the National Oceanic and Atmospheric Administration, the Environmental Protection Agency and the National Academy of Sciences. Scientists at dozens of universities have used data generated from the MBO in their research.

MT. BACHELOR TRAIL NAME ORIGINS

Many of Mt. Bachelor's trail names date back to the early days of the resort's establishment. The original Bachelor Butte trail map shows several trail names still used today, including Thunderbird, Skyliner and Tippy Toe. Thunderbird, running under the Pine Marten lift, was named after a prominent terrain feature seen on nearby Broken Top. The Skyliner run was a nod to Bend's original ski club, whose members were instrumental in establishing the resort. Tippy Toe was frequently covered in moguls and earned its name as a run that kept skiers on their toes.

Many names pay tribute to notable individuals involved with Mt. Bachelor's development and Oregon's ski culture. Two runs off the summit, Healy Heights and Beverly Hills, are named after the resort's founder, Bill Healy, and his wife, Beverly. Cliff's Run and Cliffhanger were named after Cliff Blann, who worked as mountain manager for twenty-four years and helped Bill Healy develop much of the area's early infrastructure.

Shortly after resort's first season, Bill Healy and Bradford Pease placed a statue of the Virgin Mary high in a tree along a run. The run became known as the Grotto, describing a place containing the statues of saints. Ed's Garden was supposedly named after a stubborn Forest Service landscape architect and snow ranger, Ed Fowler, who insisted that the resort leave the old tree stumps in place when developing the run in the mid-1970s.

The runs Snapshot Alley, Snapshot Bowl and Atkeson's Zoom are named after the iconic Oregon photographer Ray Atkeson, known as "the Ansel Adams of the Northwest." Atkeson began photographing western landscapes in the late 1920s. He was a charter member of the iconic Oregon

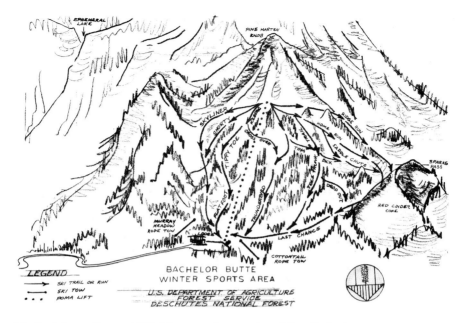

Mt. Bachelor trail map, 1958–59 season. *Image courtesy of Steve Stenkamp.*

mountaineering club the Wy'east Climbers and spent his formative years climbing Mount Hood. In the early 1930s, Atkeson met Hjalmer Hvam, future U.S. ski champion and Olympic coach. That friendship sparked his now-famous body of work focused on mountain landscapes and skiing.

In 1949, Atkeson met ski moviemaker Warren Miller in Squaw Valley. The two became friends and collaborated on the classic book *Ski & Snow Country: The Golden Years of Skiing in the West, 1930s–1950s.* Alan Engen of the Alf Engen Ski Museum at Utah Olympic Park called Atkeson "the finest ski photographer ever." Near the end of his life, Atkeson was named the photographer laureate of the state of Oregon. Several of Atkeson's photos of Mount Bachelor appear in this book, including the front cover image.

When the Outback lift on the mountain's west side was developed in the mid-1970s, many trail names played on the Australian theme, including Down Under, Bushwacker, Kangaroo, Boomerang, Melbourne and Aussie Alley.

Leeway, previously called Sparks Pass (upper segment) and Last Chance (lower segment), was renamed following the death of fifteen-year-old Lee Atherton of Roseburg, Oregon, in 1993. Atherton fell and was critically injured on the run while on a Boy Scout trip with his troop. He died several days later.

Ray Atkeson skiing with his photography equipment in the Cascade Range. *Copyright Ray Atkeson Image Archive.*

Several runs are named after prominent terrain features, such as Pinnacles, Cirque Bowl and the Moraine. Similarly, Wanoga Way is named for its exceptional views of Wanoga Butte. Sparks Lake is named for its views on the mountain's northwest side. Avalanche earned its name from its location in an old avalanche run-out zone seen in early pictures of the mountain.

Numerous runs offer nods to famous Oregon landmarks, such as I-5, Pacific City, Cannon Beach and Otter Rock. Others are named for local flora and fauna such as Hemlock, Pinecone, White Bark, Clark's Jay, Osprey Way and Brookie's Run.

The Nordic system has numerous trails and landmarks named after notable local skiers and individuals who contributed to the development of the network. A warming hut, dubbed Bob's Bungalow, is named after Bob Mathews, Mt. Bachelor's first Nordic director. Several other founding fathers are honored with trails around the network. The loop trail Woody's Way is named after Bob Woodward, who helped develop the Nordic program and was an early promoter of mountain biking in Bend. Oli's Alley is named for Dennis Oliphant, an early employee who was instrumental in developing the junior Nordic racing program.

The Nordic network's well-known gathering place, Emil's Clearing, is named after Central Oregon's iconic cross-country skier Emil Nordeen. Other trails are named in honor of noteworthy local skiers and Olympians, including Devecka's Dive, which is named after Mike Devecka, a four-time U.S. Olympic team member and the only U.S. skier to win national championships in all three Nordic disciplines. Leslie's Lunge honors Leslie Bancroft-Krichko, a two-time Olympian who trained at Mt. Bachelor.

Blue Jay's Way was named after Jay Bowerman, a two-time Olympian and U.S. champion in biathlon who trained on a makeshift biathlon course near Mount Bachelor in the late 1960s and early 1970s. Rich's Range was named after Rich Gross, a 1988 Olympic biathlon team member and head of MBSEF's biathlon training program during the late 1980s and early 1990s. Dan's Drop, formerly known as Old Maid, is named for Dan Simoneau, who was on three U.S. Olympic teams and later became the MBSEF Nordic program director.

A HISTORY OF MT. BACHELOR'S LIFTS

The 2,900-foot Poma platter-style lift was the original chair at Mt. Bachelor, built in 1958 and operated until 1964. The base was located west of Egan Lodge, running southwest to the endpoint near the Grotto. The equipment was moved to the top of Chair One (Black) in 1965 and operated there until the early 1970s.

When the resort opened, there were also two rope tows. The one-thousand-foot intermediate Cottontail rope tow was built in 1958 and was replaced with a T-bar in 1959. The endpoint of Cottontail was located to the west of the Poma lift near the water tower. The Murray Meadow rope tow was built in 1958 and operated until 1973 and was located east of Egan Lodge and west of Chair One (Black). The combined capacity of the resort's original apparatus was approximately one thousand skiers per hour.

A T-bar was built in 1959, replacing the Cottontail rope tow, east from the bottom of the Red Chair with an endpoint near the current half-pipe. It was replaced with Chair Three (Yellow) in 1967.

The 4,200-foot Riblet double chair was installed in 1961, offering a vertical rise of 1,200 feet. It was initially called the Chair and later renamed the Black Chair. The lift cost around $130,000 to purchase and install. It had 125 chairs and a capacity of around 840 skiers per hour, providing access to nine runs. The chair was located on Coffee run to the east of Egan Lodge.

The addition of the new Riblet double chair brought the resort's overall capacity to around 1,700 skiers per hour. After the bottom terminal was hit by lightning in 1974, the starting point was lowered to the base area, adding 800 feet to its length. The endpoint rose to approximately 7,700 feet, to a spot east of and slightly lower than the top of the current Pine Marten lift. The chair was removed in 1987 and sold to the Hesperus ski area near Durango, Colorado.

The Olympic rope tow was built in 1962 for the Olympic ski training area in the cirque bowl above the moraine and was used only until 1968.

Chair Two was built in 1964 close to the location of the current Red Chair. It was the second Riblet chairlift on the mountain and originally had a midway station for accessing the lower mountain used by race camps. It had a length of almost 4,000 feet, a vertical rise of 1,160 feet and the capacity to move 1,000 skiers per hour on 133 chairs. The chair was replaced in 1980 with the current Red Chair, a Yan Triple. The original Chair Two was sold to the Sitzmark Ski Area in Northern Washington.

Main Lodge rope tow was located near the West Village Lodge and was designed to provide access to the T-bar and Chair Two; it was removed in the late 1970s.

Chair Three, a double Riblet, was built in 1967 and replaced the T-bar. Its base was located east of Chair Two and followed a similar path but ended higher, near the top of the existing half-pipe. It had a length of 2,000 feet and a vertical rise of 500 feet with the capacity to move 1,200 skiers per hour on 88 chairs. The name was changed to Yellow Chair in 1973, and the terminals were replaced in 1981. The lift was removed in the early 2000s.

Mitey Mite handle tow operated for several years during the early 1970s on the east face of the Old Maid butte near the Nordic Center.

Chair Four was built in 1970 adjacent to a small day lodge. It was later renamed Blue Chair. This Riblet chair moved almost 1,200 skiers per hour along its 5,000-foot length and raised the ski area's overall capacity to over 4,100 skiers per hour. Chair Four operated until 1989 when it was replaced by the Skyliner Express. It was used as a backup chairlift until 1990.

In 1973, the naming convention for the lifts was changed from numbers to colors. Two new chairs were added that year. Chair Five, known as Orange Chair, was built near the West Village Lodge. It was Oregon's first triple chair and had the capacity to move 1,800 skiers per hour over a length of 1,500 feet. It was named Murray Meadow before installation and was removed in 1993.

A sixth chair, known as Green Chair, was also built in 1973 and followed a similar line as the current Skyliner Express but was somewhat shorter. It had the capacity to move 1,100 skiers per hours over 4,600 feet. It was initially named Button Chair and was removed in 1989 during the construction of the Skyliner Express.

The original Outback Chair was constructed in 1976 adjacent to Ed's Garden. It was the mountain's seventh Riblet chairlift. It was completed during the drought season of 1976–77 and got little use that year. Although it was replaced with a four-passenger express lift in 1987, it remained in place until 1990 as a backup chair.

The Rainbow lift, originally named Fly Creek, was completed in 1980. It was the first Yan (Lift Engineering) chairlift at Mt. Bachelor. The name was changed to Rainbow in 1981 when the Sunrise Lodge was finished. In 2016, the lift was shortened by over two thousand feet. The lift was initially known as Cloud Nine during the planning phase.

The Red Chair (originally Chair Two) was replaced in 1980 with a new Yan lift that operated along a similar path.

The original Sunrise Chair, a fixed-grip Yan triple, was built in 1981 in front of the Sunrise Lodge. Its original name during the planning phase was Quick Silver; however, its name was changed to Avalanche on completion. After the new lodge was built, the name was changed to Sunrise. The original chair was replaced in 1993 with a Doppelmayr quad detachable lift.

The Summit Chair, Bill Healy's longtime dream, was completed in 1983. During the planning phase, it was known as Silver Streak. The original lift was a Doppelmayr triple chair, one of the first detachable chairlifts in North America. It was replaced with the current quad chair in 1997.

The Pine Marten Express opened in 1986–87 to replace the old Black double chair (originally Chair One). At the time, it was the fastest chair on the mountain. It was replaced in 2006.

The Outback Express was built in 1987 and was the third high-speed detachable lift on the mountain. The opening of this chair added four new runs. A later modification moved the bottom terminal lower and to the west, while the top was extended an additional 1,500 feet up the mountain.

The Skyliner Express quad was built in 1989 to replace the Green Chair. In late 2021, the lift was out of service for the season due to mechanical problems, and it is expected to be replaced with a six-person lift. According to a press release, the new lift will be the most significant investment in a single lift in Mt. Bachelor's history and increase the old lift's capacity by 50 percent.

Sunrise Express was rebuilt in 1993 to replace the original Sunrise Triple Yan chairlift. The new Sunrise followed the same line as the original.

Alpenglow (formerly named Carrousel) was built in 1993 using parts from the original Sunrise lift.

Little Pine, a Doppelmayr quad detachable lift, was built in 1993 and replaced the Orange Chair. The bottom and top stations were moved to the east of the original Orange Chair location.

In 1996–97, Northwest Express became the westernmost lift on the mountain and opened ten new runs on the west side. Northwest Express has the most vertical feet of any lift at Mt. Bachelor. The Summit Express triple was converted to an express quad lift that same year.

The Cloudchaser lift, a Doppelmayr quad detachable costing $6.5 million, was built in 2016. The project created 6.2 miles of groomed runs and opened 635 acres of new terrain, making Mt. Bachelor the sixth-largest ski resort in the United States.

Early Riser, a Doppelmayr quad, was built in 2019. It is around 630 feet long with a capacity of 1,860 skiers per hour. The lift serves the beginner area below the Sunrise Lodge.

NOTES

Preface

1. L.A. McArthur, "Reminiscences," 73; Lent, *Central Oregon Place Names*, 174.
2. Hatton, *High Country*, 58.
3. "Mount Bachelor," *Bulletin*.
4. L.L. McArthur, "Oregon Geographic Names," 406–8.
5. Lucas, *Bill Healy's Dream*, 150.

Chapter 1

6. Miller, *Roadside Geology of Oregon*, 7.
7. U.S. Geological Survey, "Mount Bachelor."
8. Bishop and Allen, *Hiking Oregon's Geology*, 106.
9. Ewert, Diefenbach and Ramsey, "National Volcanic Threat Assessment."
10. O'Connor, "Our Vanishing Glaciers," 408.
11. Kohn, "Heatwaves, Climate Change"
12. Scott, Gardner and Sarna-Wojcicki, *Guidebook for Field Trip*, 10.
13. Phillips, "Our Vanishing Glaciers."
14. Kohn, "Shrinking Glaciers."
15. Bend–Ft. Rock Ranger District, Deschutes National Forest, *Final Environmental Impact Statement*, 13.
16. Hammers, "Record for Snow."

17. Deschutes National Forest, *Mount Bachelor Winter Interpretation Handbook*.
18. Houser, *Prehistoric Overview*, 14–26.
19. Thomas, *Oregon High*, 105.
20. Hatton, *High Country*, 79; Brogan, *Visitor Information Service Book*, 16–18.
21. Houser, *Prehistoric Overview*, 10.
22. Brogan, *Visitor Information Service Book*, 59.
23. Joslin, *Wilderness Concept*, 69.
24. Vandevert, "Vandevert Ranch History."
25. LaLande, "John B. Waldo."
26. Snead, *Oregon's John Muir*, 21.
27. Dekum, unpublished diary; Thomas, *Oregon High*, 85.
28. Dekum, unpublished diary.
29. Snead, *Oregon's John Muir*, 20.
30. Ibid., 12–14.
31. Cogswell, "Deschutes Country Pine Logging," 235–59
32. Bell, "Archaeology."
33. Joslin, *Three Sisters Wilderness*, 69.
34. Joslin, *Deschutes National Forest*, 45.
35. Cogswell, "Deschutes Country Pine Logging," 235–59.
36. Joslin, *Ponderosa Promise*, 8.
37. Briegleb, *Forest Statistics*, 6.
38. Cogswell, "Deschutes Country Pine Logging," 235.
39. Binus, "Shevlin-Hixon."
40. Stearns, "Physiography of Three Sisters," 12.
41. "Bachelor Mountain Phone Line," *Bulletin*.
42. Joslin, "Pioneering Lady Lookouts," 10.

Chapter 2

43. "Crescent," *Bulletin*; Brogan, *Visitor Information Service Book*, 138.
44. Hanson, "History of the Skyliners."
45. Albert, "Winter Comes."
46. Hanson, "Bend's Skyliners Ski Club."
47. Brauns, "Part of History."
48. Lucas, *Bill Healy's Dream*, 37.
49. Brogan, *Visitor Information Service Book*, 64.
50. Hanson, "History of the Skyliners."
51. Hanson, "Paul Hosmer."

52. Stenkamp, "Oregon Lost Ski Areas."
53. Bend Skyliners Lodge, "Nomination Form."
54. Ibid.
55. Brogan, *Visitor Information Service Book*, 111.
56. Hanson, correspondence with author.
57. Bend Skyliners Lodge, "Nomination Form."
58. Hanson, correspondence with author.
59. Hatton, *High Country*, 67.
60. "Lions to Back," *Bulletin*.
61. Stenkamp, "Lost Oregon Ski Areas."
62. "Lions to Back."
63. Hatton, *High Country*, 69.
64. B. Barber, "Bachelor Butte Area Eyed."
65. Hatton, *High Country*, 107.
66. Deschutes Historical Museum, "Look Back."
67. "Highway Department Agrees," *Bulletin*.
68. Deschutes National Forest, *Corridor Management*, 6.
69. Clark, "Gene Gillis Dies."
70. "Bill Healy," *Seattle Times*.
71. Brogan, *Visitor Information Service Book*, 139.
72. Lucas, *Bill Healy's Dream*, 81.
73. Deschutes County Historical Society, *Bend: Images of America*.
74. Hatton, *High Country*, 163.
75. Lucas, *Bill Healy's Dream*, 81.
76. Ibid., 82.
77. McDonald, "Mt. Bachelor at 50."
78. Lucas, *Bill Healy's Dream*, 79.
79. Brogan, *Visitor Information Service Book*, 139.
80. Lucas, *Bill Healy's Dream*, 93.
81. Brogan, *Visitor Information Service Book*, 89.
82. Mt. Bachelor, "Origins."
83. "Bachelor Slopes Attract," *Bulletin*; Thompson, "Bend Fast Becoming."
84. Lucas, *Bill Healy's Dream*, 100.

Chapter 3

85. Ibid., 103.
86. Riblet Tramway Company, "Riblet History."

87. Lucas, *Bill Healy's Dream*, 103–4.

88. Stenkamp, "Oregon Lost Ski Areas."

89. Waston, "Cliff Blann."

90. Hamlin, "Greatest Ski Adventure."

91. Meissner, interview with author.

92. Moore, "President Marsh Dies."

93. Lucas, *Bill Healy's Dream*, 109.

94. Ibid., 112–13.

95. Brogan, "Bachelor Proposal."

96. Raff, "He Realized Dream."

97. Stenkamp, discussions with author.

98. "Record Number of People," *Bulletin*.

99. Lucas, *Bill Healy's Dream*, 126.

100. "Skiing Set to Boom," *Bulletin*.

101. McDonald, "Mt. Bachelor at 50."

102. Shine, "Way West."

103. Joslin, "Camp Abbot."

104. Hanson, *Sunriver*, 31.

105. Sunriver Unlimited, "About Sunriver."

106. *Bulletin*, "Ceremonies to Mark."

107. U.S. Ski and Snowboard Hall of Fame, "Nelson Bennet."

108. Lucas, *Bill Healy's Dream*, 127.

109. Ibid., 128.

110. Stenkamp, "Oregon Lost Ski Areas."

111. Ibid.

112. Battistella, "Tucker Sno-Cat®."

113. Armpriest, "Cross Country Ski Centers," 130–55.

114. Meissner, interview with author.

115. Carroll and Flowers, "Outdoor Pioneers."

116. Bowerman, interview with author.

117. Nakamura, "True Trailblazer."

118. Mathews, interviews and correspondence with author.

119. Armpriest, "Cross Country Ski Centers."

120. Roozen, "First Tracks."

121. Armpriest, "Cross Country Ski Centers."

122. Woodward, interview with author.

123. Portman, "Bob Woodward Inducted."

124. Oliphant, interview with author.

125. Hoyt, "Virginia Meissner."

126. "Jack Meissner," *Bulletin*.

127. Lucas, *Bill Healy's Dream*, 129.

128. Brooks Resource Corporation.

129. Lucas, *Bill Healy's Dream*, 142.

Chapter 4

130. Deschutes National Forest, *Environmental Assessment*, 1.

131. Ibid., 4.

132. Ibid., 127.

133. Ibid., 13.

134. Lucas, *Bill Healy's Dream*, 132.

135. Deschutes National Forest, *Environmental Assessment*, 133.

136. Ibid., 14.

137. Mt. Bachelor Inc., "Financing—The Big Issue."

138. Deschutes National Forest, "Mount Bachelor Plan Approved."

139. Lucas, *Bill Healy's Dream*, 142.

140. Kagan, "Wilderness, Luck & Love."

141. Lucas, *Bill Healy's Dream*, 143.

142. Deschutes National Forest, *Environmental Assessment*, 3–28.

143. Lucas, *Bill Healy's Dream*, 152.

144. Ibid., 151.

145. Ibid., 140.

146. Barton, "Out-of-Staters Visit."

147. Darling, "Pine Marten Lodge."

148. Kirby Nagelhout Construction Company, "Pine Marten Lodge."

149. McDonald, "Mount Bachelor at 50."

150. Lucas, *Bill Healy's Dream*, 164.

151. Ibid., 154.

152. Ibid., 158

153. Ibid., 163.

154. Ibid., 177.

155. "Bill Healy," *Seattle Times*.

156. C. Barker, "Bridge to Be Named."

157. Neilson, "Chief Owner against Sale."

158. Lucas, *Bill Healy's Dream*, 192.

159. Moore, "President Marsh Dies."

Chapter 5

160. RCC Associates, *End of Season Survey*.
161. D. Thompson, "No Business."
162. Community Planning Workshop, *Oregon Skier Profile*.
163. Rathbun, interview with author.
164. Fisher, "Mt. Bachelor Land."
165. Cumming, "John Cumming."
166. Benson and Robinson, "Ian Cumming."
167. Barco, "Bachelor Owner Outlines Plans."
168. "Utah Firm Poised," *Eugene Register-Guard*.
169. B. Miller, "Mt. Bachelor Ski Resort."
170. Papé, Letter to Mt. Bachelor shareholders.
171. Neilson, "Chief Owner against Sale."
172. McDonald, "Mt. Bachelor at 50."
173. "Utah Firm Poised."
174. Barco, "Bachelor Owner Outlines Plans."
175. Max, "Breaking Point."
176. Fisher, "Mt. Bachelor Land."
177. Max, "Breaking Point."
178. Lomax, correspondence with author.
179. Daniel, "U.S. Ski Industry," 262–85.
180. Hamway, "Good Bargain for Skiing?"
181. McDonald, "Bachelor Names New President."
182. "Ski Resort Responds," Associated Press.
183. McDonald, "Mt. Bachelor at 50."
184. Kray, "Master Plan Approval."
185. Hyatt, "Sales Decline Prompts."
186. Hammers, "President Is Out."
187. Ecosign Mountain Resort Planners, *Master Development Plan*.
188. Kray, "Master Plan Approval."
189. Ecosign Mountain Resort Planners, *Master Development Plan*, I-2.
190. Rathbun, interview with author.
191. Wesseler, correspondence and discussions with author.
192. "Slippery Slope to Success," *Bend Source*.
193. U.S. Department of Agriculture, "U.S. Forest Service Finalizes."
194. M. Barber, "New Boom Season."
195. EPR Properties, "Ski Resorts in Summer."

196. Bend–Ft. Rock Ranger District, Deschutes National Forest, *Final Environmental Impact Statement*.
197. "Mt. Bachelor Plans," *Oregonian*.
198. "Powdr Acquires," *Cascade Business News*.
199. McLaughlin, "Zip Line."
200. Spurr, "Mt. Bachelor to Build."

Chapter 6

201. Lucas, *Bill Healy's Dream*, 79.
202. Brogan, *Visitor Information Service Book*, 139.
203. Anderson, *Objective in Mind*, 409.
204. Max, "Breaking Point."
205. Hopper, "Use of Dry Well"; Lucas, *Bill Healy's Dream*, 115.
206. Lucas, *Bill Healy's Dream*, 112.
207. Ibid., 142.
208. Deschutes National Forest, *Environmental Assessment*, 130.
209. "Don Peters Recipient of Rescue Award," *Bulletin*.
210. Lucas, *Bill Healy's Dream*, 98.
211. Peters, "From Howitzers to Hotlines."
212. Wesseler, correspondence and discussions with author.
213. U.S. Department of Agriculture, "Chronology."
214. Wilkinson, "Greatest Good," 72.
215. Pinchot, *National Forests*, 24.
216. Waugh, *Recreation Uses*, 1–37.
217. Ibid., 3.
218. Hale, "Now 100 Years Old."
219. Briggs, "Ski Resorts," 89.
220. Deschutes National Forest, *Winter Interpretation Handbook*, 10.
221. S. Barker, "Oregon Skyline Trail," 46–73.
222. Mark, "Frederick William Cleator."
223. Arave, "Takes to the Slopes," 342.
224. Vora, "Recreational Residence Program," 18–19.
225. Tweed, *History of Outdoor Recreation*, 24.
226. Lewis, *Forest Service*, 126.
227. T. Thompson, "New Winter Spirit."
228. Childers, "Fire on the Mountain," 18.
229. Williams, "Forest Era," 46.

230. Rockefeller, *Outdoor Recreation for America*.
231. Williams, "Forest Era," 102–11.
232. Ruckriegle, Mercer and Fugere, "Hotspots in Wildfire Risk," 34.
233. McKinzie, "Ski Area Development," 299.
234. Ibid., 299–328.
235. Ruckriegle, Mercer and Fugere, "Hotspots in Wildfire Risk," 29; Briggs, "Ski Resorts," 94.
236. U.S. Forest Service, Ski Area Permits.
237. Keller, "Rules Catch Up."
238. U.S. Forest Service, "Proposed Directive."
239. Tidwell, speech to the National Ski Area Association.
240. Laitos and Carr, "Transformation on Public Lands,"160–62.
241. Christiansen, speech to the National Ski Area Association.
242. Peters, "Future of Ski Resorts."
243. Christiansen, speech to the National Ski Area Association.
244. "Pay Cheap Rent," *Rutland Herald*.
245. Blevins, "Ski Resorts Send."
246. Briggs, "Ski Resorts," 89.
247. Deschutes National Forest, *Sustainability Analysis*.
248. U.S. Forest Service, "Master Development Plans."
249. Bend–Ft. Rock Ranger District, *Final Environmental Impact Statement*, S-1.
250. Lovett, "Role of the Forest Service."
251. Sherman, Neslin and Whitlock, "Ski Development."
252. Briggs, "Ski Resorts," 97.
253. Hansman, "Drawing the Line," 4–5.
254. Berwyn, "Ski Industry Takes Aim."
255. Kray, "Master Plan Approval."
256. Wesseler, interview with the author, and Lomax, interview with the author.

Chapter 7

257. Hanson, "History of the Skyliners."
258. Gibbons, "Fort Klamath to Crater Lake."
259. Hanson, "History of the Skyliners."
260. Ibid.
261. Hatton, *High Country*, 67.
262. Stenkamp, "Lost Oregon Ski Areas."
263. Ruble, "Coach Beattie, Olympic Skiers."

264. Nelson, "Lost Ski Areas."

265. Cammack, interview with author.

266. "U.S. Nationals Invade," *Bulletin*.

267. Anstine, "Lafferty Enjoying."

268. Oliphant, interview with author.

269. Bowerman, interview with author.

270. Madsen, "Central Oregon Lacks."

271. Ridler, "Bachelor Lands."

Chapter 8

272. Deschutes National Forest, *Annual Report*.

273. Roig, "Oregon's Visitor Numbers Grow."

274. Deschutes National Forest, *Annual Report*.

275. Dalton and Fleishman, *Fifth Oregon Climate Assessment*, 7–8.

276. Halofsky, Peterson and Ho, *Climate Change Vulnerability*, 59.

277. Kohn, "Heatwaves, Climate Change."

278. Barr et al., *Projected Future Conditions*, 23.

279. Halofsky, Peterson and Ho, *Climate Change Vulnerability*, 58.

280. Ibid., 76.

281. Capalbo et al., "Climate Change in Oregon," 361.

282. Hagenstad, Burakowski and Hill, *Economic Contributions*, 5–6.

283. Steiger et al., "Climate Change Risk," 1343–45.

284. Burakowski and Magnusson, *Climate Impacts*, 18–19.

285. Ibid., 15.

286. Madsen, "Climate Change Could."

287. Community Planning Workshop, *Oregon Skier Profile*, 13–25.

288. Jaffe, correspondence with author.

289. Farley et al., "Persistent Influence," 3645–57.

BIBLIOGRAPHY

Books and Monographs

Anderson, Rolf. *We Had an Objective in Mind: The U.S. Forest Service in the Pacific Northwest 1905 to 2005: A Centennial Anthology*. Portland, OR: Pacific Northwest Forest Service Association, 2005.

Bishop, Ellen Morris, and John Eliot Allen. *Hiking Oregon's Geology*. Seattle, WA: Mountaineers, 1996.

Cogswell, P., Jr. "Deschutes Country Pine Logging." In *High and Mighty: Selected Sketches about the Deschutes Country*, edited by T. Vaughn, 235–59. Portland: Oregon Historical Society, 1981.

Daniel, Scott. "U.S. Ski Industry Adaptation to Climate Change: Hard, Soft and Policy Strategies." In *Tourism and Global Environmental Change*, edited by Stefan Gössling and Michael C. Hall. London: Routledge, 2005.

Deschutes County Historical Society. *Bend: Images of America*. Charleston, SC: Arcadia, 2009.

Hanson, Tor. *Sunriver*. Charleston, SC: Arcadia, 2018.

Hatton, Raymond R. *High Country of Central Oregon*. Portland, OR: Binford & Mort, 1977.

Joslin, Les. *Deschutes National Forest*. Charleston, SC: Arcadia, 2017.

———. *Three Sisters Wilderness: A History*. Charleston, SC: The History Press, 2021.

———. *The Wilderness Concept and the Three Sisters Wilderness*. Bend, OR: Wilderness Associates, 2005.

Kriegh, LeeAnn. *The Nature of Bend*. Bend, OR: Tempo Press, 2016.

Lent, Steve. *Deschutes County*. Vol. 3 of *Central Oregon Place Names*. Deschutes County, OR: Crook County Historical Society, 2015.

Lewis, James G. *The Forest Service and the Greatest Good: A Centennial History*. Durham, NC: Forest History Society, 2005.

Lucas, Peggy Chessman. *Mt. Bachelor: Bill Healy's Dream; History and Development of the Mt. Bachelor Ski Resort*. Bend, OR: Maverick, 1999.

Miller, Marli B. *Roadside Geology of Oregon*. Missoula, MT: Mountain Press, 2014.

Snead, Bobbie. *Judge John B. Waldo: Oregon's John Muir*. Bend, OR: Maverick, 2006.

Steen, Harold K. *The U.S. Forest Service: A History*. Seattle, WA: University of Washington Press, 1976.

Thomas, Jeff. *Oregon High: A Climbing Guide to Nine Cascade Volcanoes*. Portland, OR: Keep Climbing Press, 1991.

Periodicals and Newsletters

Albert, Jason. "Winter Comes: Oregon's Nordic Ski History on Exhibit." *Fast Skier*, October 2016.

Arave, Joseph. "The Forest Service Takes to the Slopes: The Birth of Utah's Ski Industry and the Role of the Forest Service." *Utah Historical Quarterly* 70. no. 4 (Fall 2002).

Barber, Megan. "Why Summer Is the New Boom Season for Ski Towns." *Curbed*, July 27, 2017.

Barker, Stuart. "The Oregon Skyline Trail: Evolving Attitudes toward Nature Tourism." *Oregon Historical Quarterly* 120, no. 1 (Spring 2019).

Briggs, James. "Ski Resorts and the National Forests: Rethinking Forest Service Management Practices for Recreational Use." *Boston College Environmental Affairs Law Review* 28, no. 1 (2000).

Carroll, Cathy, and Eric Flowers. "Outdoor Pioneers." *Bend Magazine*, April 2016. https://bendmagazine.com/founders/

Charest, Dalton. "Dan Simoneau Is Ready to Get Back on the Snow." *Bend Magazine*, January 2019.

Farley, Ryan, et al. "Persistent Influence of Wildfire Emissions in the Western United States and Characteristics of Aged Biomass Burning Organic Aerosols under Clean Air Conditions." *Environmental Science & Technology* 56, no. 6 (2022), 3645–57.

Hamlin, Annemarie. "The Greatest Ski Adventure." *1859 Magazine*, January 2010.

Hansman, Heather. "Drawing the Line." *Trail Break: Winter Wildlands Alliance Newsletter*, Fall 2021.

Hanson, Tor. "The Legacy of Bend's Skyliners Ski Club Lives On." *Bend Magazine*, January 2021.

———. "Paul Hosmer, the Bard of Bend." *Bend Magazine*, March 2018.

Joslin, Les. "Pioneering Lady Lookouts of the U.S. Forest Service." *OldSmokeys Newsletter*, Summer 2018.

Kagan, Neil. "Wilderness, Luck & Love: A Memoir and a Tribute." *Michigan Journal of Environmental & Administrative Law* 7, no 2 (2018).

Keller, Sarah Jane. "Forest Service Rules Catch Up with the Growth of Year-Round Activities at Ski Resorts." *High County News*, October 2013.

Kray, Peter. "Master Plan Approval Great for Bachelor, but not a Precedent." *Outside Business Journal*, February 2011.

Laitos, Jan G., and Thomas A. Carr. "The Transformation on Public Lands." *Ecology Law Quarterly* 26, no. 2 (1999).

Lovett, Richard A. "The Role of the Forest Service in Ski Resort Development: An Economic Approach to Public Lands Management." *Ecology Law Quarterly* 10, no. 4 (1983).

Max, Kevin. "Breaking Point." *Bend Business Review* 1, no. 2 (2007–8).

McArthur, Lewis L. "Oregon Geographic Names." *Oregon Historical Quarterly* 85, no. 4 (1984).

McArthur, Lewis A. "Reminiscences of John Y. Todd." *Oregon Historical Quarterly* 30, no. 1 (1929).

McKinzie, Wayne C. "Ski Area Development after the National Forest Ski Area Permit Act of 1986: Still an Uphill Battle." *Virginia Environmental Law Journal* 12, no. 2 (1993).

Nelson, Noah. "The Lost Ski Areas of Central Oregon." *Bend Magazine*, November 2021.

O'Connor, Jim E. "Our Vanishing Glaciers: One Hundred Years of Glacier Retreat in Three Sisters Area, Oregon Cascade Range." *Oregon Historical Quarterly* 114, no. 4 (Winter 2013).

Peters, Greg M. "From Howitzers to Hotlines." *National Forest Foundation*, Winter/Spring 2015.

———. "The Future of Ski Resorts on Public Lands." *National Forest Foundation*, Winter/Spring 2014.

Portman, Don. "Bob Woodward Inducted into Mountain Bike Hall of Fame." *SkiTrax*, December 21, 2012.

Ruckriegle, Heidi, Lauren Mercer and Leah Fugere. "Hotspots in Wildfire Risk at Public Lands Ski Areas." *Colorado Lawyer*, February 2021.

Steiger, Robert, Daniel Scott, Bruno Abegg, Marc Pons and Carlo Aall. "A Critical Review of Climate Change Risk for Ski Tourism." *Current Issues in Tourism* 22, no. 11 (2019).

Thompson, Derek. "No Business like Snow Business: The Economics of Big Ski Resorts." *Atlantic*, February 2012.

Thompson, Tom L. "A New Winter Spirit for the Outfit: The Story of Skiing on the National Forests." *National Museum of Forest Service History* 34, no. 1 (Winter 2022).

Wilkinson, Charles. "'Greatest Good of the Greatest Number in the Long Run': TR, Pinchot, and the Origins of Sustainability in America." *Colorado National Resources, Energy, and Environmental Law Review* 26, no. 1 (2015).

Newspapers

Anstine, Dennis. "Lafferty Enjoying Some 'Home' Skiing." *Bulletin* (Bend, OR), March 8, 1972.

Associated Press. "Mt. Bachelor Ski Resort Responds to Complaints." April 13, 2008.

Barber, Bob. "Bachelor Butte Area Eyed as Sports Site." *Bulletin* (Bend, OR), February 27, 1957.

Barco, Torri. "Bachelor Owner Outlines Plans." *Bulletin* (Bend, OR), June 19, 2001.

Barker, Chris. "Bridge to Be Named after Ski Resort Founder." *Bulletin* (Bend, OR), October 16, 2003.

Barton, Gene. "More Out-of-Staters Visit." *Bulletin* (Bend, OR), November 6, 1983.

Bend Source (Bend, OR). "The Slippery Slope to Success." October 26, 2011.

Benson, Lee, and Doug Robinson. "Ian Cumming Lived Life with Little Fanfare and Died the Same Way." *Deseret News* (Salt Lake City, UT), February 7, 2018.

Berwyn, Bob. "Ski Industry Takes Aim at NEPA Reform." *Vail Daily* (Vail, CO), January 14, 2010.

Blevins, Jason. "Ski Resorts Send a Record-Setting Rent Payment to the Federal Government after 2017–18 Season." *Colorado Sun* (Denver, CO), June 13, 2019.

Brauns, Katie. "A Part of History: Annual Great Nordeen Cross-Country Ski Race Links the Past to the Present." *Bulletin* (Bend, OR), December 16, 2007.

Brogan, Phil. "Bachelor Proposal Has 100 Per Cent Business Support." *Bulletin* (Bend, OR), May 16, 1964.

Bulletin (Bend, OR). "Bachelor Mountain Phone Line Ready." September 22, 1922.

———. "Bachelor Slopes Attract 36,000 Skiers for Season." June 28, 1960.

———. "Ceremonies to Mark New Road Opening." November 16, 1983.

———. "Crescent." February 4, 1914.

———. "Don Peters Recipient of Rescue Award." April 6, 1962.

———. "Highway Department Agrees to Ski Road Snow Removal." August 30, 1966.

———. "Jack Meissner Obituary." November 19, 2008.

———. "Lions to Back Bend Ski Club." November 25, 1946.

———. "Mount Bachelor." August 18, 1955.

———. "Record Number of People Use Ski Area at Bachelor Butte." May 4, 1966.

———. "Skiing Set to Boom." November 21, 1970.

Cascade Business News (Bend, OR). "Powdr Acquires Central Oregon Adventure Outfitter Sun Country Tours." June 14, 2016.

Clark, Heather. "Central Oregon Skiing Pioneer Gene Gillis Dies." *Bulletin* (Bend, OR), December 16, 2005.

Darling, Dylan J. "Pine Marten Lodge: Quick Design and Build." *Bulletin* (Bend, OR), December 5, 2015.

Deschutes Historical Museum. "A Look Back: Mt. Bachelor Resort, Century Drive." *Bend Bulletin* (Bend, OR), December 8, 2019.

Deschutes National Forest. "Mount Bachelor Plan Approved." *Forest Service News* (April 28, 1981).

Fisher, David. "Mt. Bachelor Land for Sale." *Bulletin* (Bend, OR), October 31, 2005.

Hale, Jamie. "Now 100 Years Old, Eagle Creek Helped Revolutionize Camping in the 20th Century." *Oregonian* (Portland, OR), July 14, 2016.

Hammers, Scott. "Mt. Bachelor President Is Out." *Bulletin* (Bend, OR), March 17, 2016.

———. "Mount Bachelor Sets a Record for Snow." *Bulletin* (Bend, OR), April 29, 2011.

Hamway, Stephen. "Is Mt. Bachelor a Good Bargain for Skiing?" *Bulletin* (Bend, OR), October 23, 2016.

Hanson, Tor. "The History of the Skyliners." *Bulletin* (Bend, OR), January 19, 2019.

Hopper, Grant. "Use of Dry Well Denied by Officials." *Bulletin* (Bend, OR), December 29, 1965.

Hyatt, Abraham. "Sales Decline Prompts Mt. Bachelor Shakeup." *Oregon Business* (Portland, OR), June 30, 2008.

Kirk, Andrew. "Power Acquires Camp Woodward." *Park Record* (Park, City, UT) July 29, 2011.

Kohn, Michael. "Heatwaves, Climate Change Pushing Central Oregon Glaciers Closer to Extinction." *Bulletin* (Bend, OR), February 7, 2022.

———. "Shrinking Glaciers Could Impact Life in Central Oregon." *Bulletin* (Bend, OR), April 28, 2020.

Kray, Peter. "Master Plan Approval Great for Bachelor, but Not a Precedent." *Outside Business Journal*, February 15, 2011.

Lorentz, Karen. "Power Restructuring; Acquisitions Focus on Adventure Lifestyle." *Mountain Times* (Killington, VT), May 24, 2017.

Madsen, Peter. "Central Oregon Lacks a Biathlon Scene." *Bulletin* (Bend, OR), January 31, 2020.

———. "Climate Change Could More Than Halve Mt. Bachelor Ski Season." *Bulletin* (Bend, OR), September 29, 2018.

McDonald, Jeff. "Bachelor Names New President." *Bulletin* (Bend, OR), May 23, 2007.

———. "Mt. Bachelor at 50." *Bulletin* (Bend, OR), November 30, 2008.

McLaughlin, Kathleen. "Zip Line Part of Mt. Bachelor's Quest to Become a Year-Round Destination." *Bulletin* (Bend, OR), August 4, 2019.

Miller, Brian K. "Mt. Bachelor Ski Resort Board of Directors Rejects Purchase Offer at First Meeting." GlobeSt.com, January 9, 2001.

Moore, Jason. "Former Bachelor President Marsh Dies." *Bulletin* (Bend, OR), January 17, 2001.

Nakamura, Penny. "A True Trailblazer: Bob Mathews, Mount Bachelor's Nordic Pioneer, Helped Put Central Oregon on the Map as a World-Class Cross-Country Destination." *Bulletin* (Bend, OR), January 22, 2011.

———. "What's in a Name?" *Bulletin* (Bend, OR), March 5, 2006.

Neilson, Jeff. "Chief Owner against Sale of Bachelor." *Bulletin* (Bend, OR), January 7, 2001.

Oregonian (Portland, OR). "Mt. Bachelor Plans to Add Mountain Park and Remodel Lodge." June 18, 2019.

Raff, Lily. "He Realized Dream of Bachelor Resort." *Bulletin* (Bend, OR), April 24, 2004.

Ridler, Keith. "Bachelor Lands Olympic Qualifying Events." *Bulletin* (Bend, OR), October 22, 2001.

Roig, Suzanne. "Oregon's Visitor Numbers Grow." *Bulletin* (Bend, OR), May 7, 2020.

Roozen, Taylor. "First Tracks: Bob Mathews and the History of Mount Bachelor Nordic Skiing." *Source Weekly* (Bend, OR), February 7, 2013.

Ruble, Web. "Coach Beattie, Olympic Skiers Well Pleased by Bachelor Area." *Bulletin* (Bend, OR), August 27, 1963.

Rutland Herald (Rutland, VT). "Ski Areas Pay Cheap Rent for Federal Lands." October 17, 2018.

Seattle (WA) Times. "Bill Healy; Built Mount Bachelor Ski Resort." October 29, 1993.

Spurr, Kyle. "Mt. Bachelor to Build New Summit Hiking, Biking Trail." *Bulletin* (Bend, OR), May 22, 2021.

Thompson, Bill. "Bend Fast Becoming Winter Sports Hub." *Bulletin* (Bend, OR), December 13, 1960.

"U.S. Nationals Invade Mt. Bachelor Tomorrow." *Bulletin* (Bend, OR), March 8, 1972.

"Utah Firm Poised to Buy Bachelor." *Eugene Register-Guard* (Eugene, OR), March 21, 2001.

Documents and Reports

Armpriest, Diane. "Cross Country Ski Centers: Designing for a High-Quality Recreation Experience." Master's thesis, Department of Landscape Architecture, University of Oregon, June 1984.

Barr, Brian R., et al. *Projected Future Conditions and Sector Background Information for the Deschutes River Basin of Central Oregon*. Ashland, OR: Geos Institute, 2011.

Bend–Ft. Rock Ranger District, Deschutes National Forest. *Final Environmental Impact Statement: Mt. Bachelor Ski Area Improvements Project*. Washington, D.C.: U.S. Forest Service, February 2013.

Bend Skyliners Lodge. "National Register of Historic Places Inventory Nomination Form." Washington, D.C.: U.S. Department of the Interior, March 1978.

Briegleb, Philip A. *Forest Statistics for Deschutes County, Oregon*. Portland, OR: U.S. Department of Agriculture, Forest Service, Pacific Northwest Forest Experiment Station, 1936.

Brogan, Phil F. *Visitor Information Service Book for the Deschutes National Forest.* Washington, D.C.: U.S. Department of Agriculture, 1969.

Burakowski, Elizabeth, and Matthew Magnusson. *Climate Impacts on the Winter Tourism Economy in the United States.* Protect Our Winters and Natural Resources Defense Council, 2012.

Capalbo, S., J. Julian, T. Maness and E. Kelly. "Toward Assessing the Economic Impact of Climate Change in Oregon." In *Oregon Climate Assessment Report*, edited by K.D. Dello and P.W. Mote. Corvallis, OR: Oregon Climate Change Research Institute, Oregon State University, 2010.

Childers, Michael W. "Fire on the Mountain: Growth and Conflict in Colorado Ski Country." PhD diss., University of Nevada, Las Vegas, 2010.

Christiansen, Vicki. Speech to the National Ski Area Association/Forest Service Summit Lake Tahoe, California. January 14, 2020.

Coe, Daniel E. *Three Sisters Geologic Guide and Recreation Map.* Salem, OR: Oregon Department of Geology and Mineral Industries, 2012.

Community Planning Workshop. *Oregon Skier Profile and Economic Impact Analysis.* Eugene, OR: University of Oregon Community Service Center, December 2012.

Dalton, Meghan, and Erica Fleishman, eds. *Fifth Oregon Climate Assessment.* Corvallis, OR: Oregon Climate Change Research Institute, 2021.

Dekum, Adolph. Unpublished diary of 1883 trip through the Cascades with Judge John Breckenridge Waldo. Courtesy of Jeff Thomas.

Deschutes National Forest. *Annual Report, 2018–2019.* Washington, D.C.: United States Department of Agriculture, 2019.

———. *Corridor Management & Interpretive Plan.* Washington: D.C.: U.S. Department of Agriculture, 2018.

———. *Environmental Assessment Mount Bachelor Master Plan: Decision Notice and Finding of No Significant Effect.* Washington: D.C.: U.S. Department of Agriculture, April 29, 1981.

———. *Land Management Plan Environmental Impact Statement.* Washington, D.C.: United States Department of Agriculture, 1977.

———. *Mount Bachelor Winter Interpretation Handbook, 2000/2001 Season.* Washington, D.C.: United States Department of Agriculture, 1977.

———. *Winter Recreation Sustainability Analysis.* Washington, D.C.: United States Department of Agriculture, August 2009.

Diethelm and Bressler, Inc. *Mt. Bachelor Recreation Area: Proposed Preliminary Master Plan.* Eugene, OR: n.p., January 1980.

Ecosign Mountain Resort Planners. *Mount Bachelor Master Development Plan.* Whistler, BC: Ecosign Mountain Resort Planners, 2010.

EPR Properties. *Ski Resorts in Summer: Leveraging Opportunity.* August 2015.

Ewert, J.W., A.K. Diefenbach and D.W. Ramsey. *Update to the U.S. Geological Survey National Volcanic Threat Assessment.* Washington, D.C.: U.S. Geological Survey, 2018.

Frankson, R., K.E. Kunkel, S.M. Champion, L.E. Stevens, D.R. Easterling, K. Dello, M. Dalton, D. Sharp and L. O'Neill. *Oregon State Climate Summary 2022.* NOAA Technical Report NESDIS 150-OR. Silver Spring, MD: NOAA/NESDIS, 2022.

Gardner, Cynthia A. *Temporal, Spatial and Petrologic Variations of Lava Flows from the Mount Bachelor Volcanic Chain, Central Oregon High Cascades.* Vancouver, WA: U.S. Geological Survey, 1994.

Hagenstad, M., E.A. Burakowski and R. Hill. *Economic Contributions of Winter Sports in a Changing Climate.* Boulder, CO: Protect Our Winters, 2018.

Halofsky, Jessica E., David L. Peterson and Joanne J. Ho, eds. *Climate Change Vulnerability and Adaptation in South-Central Oregon.* Portland, OR: Pacific Northwest Research Station, 2019.

Houser, Michael. *A Prehistoric Overview of Deschutes County.* Bend, OR: Deschutes County Community Development Department, 1996.

Joslin, Les. *Ponderosa Promise: A History of the U.S. Forest Service Research in Central Oregon.* Washington, D.C.: United States Department of Agriculture, 2007.

Mt. Bachelor, Inc. "Financing—The Big Issue." Undated press release, circa 1980.

Papé, Randy C. Letter to Mt. Bachelor shareholders, January 10, 2001. Deschutes County Historical Society.

Phillips, Kenneth N. "Our Vanishing Glaciers: Observations by Mazamas Research Committee on Glaciers of the Cascade Range in Oregon." *Mazama* 20, no. 12 (1938).

Pinchot, Gifford. *The Use of the National Forests.* Washington, D.C.: U.S. Department of Agriculture, Forest Service, 1907.

RCC Associates. *Kottke National End of Season Survey 2008/09.* Lakewood, CO: National Ski Areas Association, 2009.

Rockefeller, Laurance S. *Outdoor Recreation for America. A Report to the President and to the Congress by the Outdoor Recreation Resources Review Commission.* Washington, D.C.: Government Printing Office, January 1962.

Royce, Charles C., and Cyrus Thomas. *Indian Land Cessions in the United States.* 1899. Library of Congress. https://www.loc.gov/item/13023487/.

Scott, William E., Cynthia A. Gardner and Andrei M. Sarna-Wojcicki. *Guidebook for Field Trip to the Mount Bachelor—South Sister—Bend Area, Central Oregon High Cascades*. Washington, D.C.: Department of the Interior, U.S. Geological Survey, 1989.

Sherman, Harris D., David S. Neslin and Ian K. Whitlock. "Ski Development in National Forests." Paper presented at the Public Lands During the Remainder of the 20th Century: Planning, Law, and Policy in the Federal Land Agencies (Summer Conference, June 8–10, 1987).

Stearns, Jane. "Physiography of Three Sisters." In *A Record of Mountaineering in the Pacific Northwest*. Portland, OR: James, Kerns & Abbott, 1912.

Tidwell, Tom. Speech to the National Ski Area Association, Public Lands Committee, Scottsdale, Arizona. May 5, 2017.

Tweed, William C. *A History of Outdoor Recreation Development in the National Forests: 1891–1942*. Washington, D.C.: U.S. Department of Agriculture, 1989.

U.S. Department of Agriculture. "U.S. Forest Service Finalizes Policy to Promote Year-Round Recreation on Ski Areas." Washington, D.C.: Office of Communications, April 15, 2015.

U.S. Forest Service. "Proposed Directive for Additional Seasonal or Year-Round Recreation Activities at Ski Areas." *Federal Register* 78, no. 191 (October 2013), 60816–20.

U.S. Forest Service. Ski Area Permits, 53 Fed. Reg. 40739 (18 October 1988); National Forest Ski Area Permit Act of 1986, Pub. L. No. 99–522 (S 2266), 100 Stat. 3000 (1986).

Vora, Rachel. "The History of the Recreational Residence Program on the Deschutes National Forest." Undergraduate thesis, University of Oregon, 2009.

Waldo, John Breckenridge. *Diaries and Letters from the High Cascades of Oregon, 1880–1907*. Edited by Gerald W. Williams. Washington, D.C.: Umpqua and Willamette National Forests, 1985.

Waston, John. "Cliff Blann: Far West Service Award Citation." Far West Ski Association, 2014.

Waugh, Frank Albert. *Recreation Uses on the National Forests*. Washington, D.C.: U.S. Government Printing Office, 1918.

Williams, Gerald W. "The Fully Managed, Multiple-Use Forest Era, 1960–1970." In *The USDA Forest Service: The First Century*. Washington, D.C.: USDA Forest Service Office of Communication, 2006.

William Wilson and Associates. *Mt Bachelor Ski Area Development Plan*. Eugene, OR: June 1969.

Digital Resources and Websites

Battistella, Edwin. "Tucker Sno-Cat®." Oregon Encyclopedia. March 17, 2018. https://www.oregonencyclopedia.org/articles/tucker_sno_cat_/.

Bell, Caitlin. "Archaeology of the Lakes Basin." Oregon Explorer: Natural Resources Digital Library. https://oregonexplorer.info/content/archaeology-the-lakes-basin.

Binus, Joshua. "Shevlin-Hixon and Brooks-Scanlon Mills." Oregon Historical Society, 2005. https://www.oregonhistoryproject.org/articles/historical-records/shevlin-hixon-and-brooks-scanlon-mills-bend/.

Brock, Mathew, and John Jack Grauer. "Mazamas." Oregon Encyclopedia, March 31, 2021. https://www.oregonencyclopedia.org/articles/mazamas/.

Brooks Resource Corporation. https://brooksresources.com.

Cole, Tara. "Capturing a Winter Wonderland: Photography by Ray Atkeson." Oregon Historical Society. March 8, 2022. https://www.ohs.org/blog/capturing-a-winter-wonderland-ray-atkeson.cfm.

Cumming, John. "John Cumming: Passion for Utah and Outdoors" (transcript of interview with Tom Kelly). Last Chair: The Ski Utah Podcast, October 27, 2020. https://www.skiutah.com/blog/authors/tom-kelly/john-cumming-passion-for-utah-and.

Forest Lookouts. "Bachelor Butte: Deschutes National Forest 18S-9E-31." https://oregonlookouts.weebly.com/bachelor-butte.html.

Gibbons, Tim. "Fort Klamath to Crater Lake Ski Race, 1927–1938." Oregon Encyclopedia. July 12, 2021. https://www.oregonencyclopedia.org/articles/fort_klamath_to_crater_lake_race/.

Hoyt, Ron. "Virginia Meissner: A Lasting Legacy." Meissner Nordic Ski Club. 2011. https://meissnernordic.org/virginia-meissner.

Johnson, Karen K. "Black Butte Ranch." Oregon Encyclopedia. April 2, 2021. https://www.oregonencyclopedia.org/articles/black_butte_ranch/.

Joslin, Les. "Camp Abbot." Oregon Encyclopedia. September 4, 2018. https://www.oregonencyclopedia.org/articles/camp_abbot/.

———. "Elk Lake Guard Station." Oregon Encyclopedia, 2014. https://www.oregonencyclopedia.org/articles/elk_lake_guard_station/.

Kirby Nagelhout Construction Company. "Pine Marten Lodge at Mt. Bachelor." https://kirbynagelhout.com/portfolio-item/pine-marten-lodge-at-mount-bachelor.

LaLande, Jeff. "John B. Waldo (1844–1907)." Oregon Encyclopedia. March 24, 2022. https://www.oregonencyclopedia.org/articles/waldo_john_b_1844_1907_/.

Mark, Stephen R. "Frederick William Cleator (1883–1957)." Oregon Encyclopedia. December 16, 2021. https://www.oregonencyclopedia.org/articles/cleator-fred/.

———. "William Gladstone Steel." Oregon Encyclopedia. November 14, 2021. https://www.oregonencyclopedia.org/articles/steel_william_1854_1934_/.

Miller, Chris. "History." Cascade Ski Club and Lodge. https://www.cascadeskiclub.org/content/history.aspx.

Mt. Bachelor. "Origins." https://www.mtbachelor.com/culture/outplay-culture/origins

Mt. Hood Skibowl. "Mt Hood Skibowl History." https://www.skibowl.com/about-skibowl/history.html.

Riblet Tramway Company. "Riblet History." https://www.riblet.com/history.htm.

Shine, Gregory P. "The Way West (Film)." Oregon Encyclopedia. April 7, 2022. https://www.oregonencyclopedia.org/articles/the_way_west_film/.

Stenkamp, Steve. "Lost Oregon Ski Areas." Facebook. https://www.facebook.com/lostoregonskiareas/.

Sunriver Unlimited. "About Sunriver." http://www.sunriverunlimited.com/aboutsr/.

U.S. Department of Agriculture. "Chronology of National Forest Management Laws and Regulations." https://www.fs.usda.gov/Internet/FSE_DOCUMENTS/fseprd530507.pdf.

U.S. Forest Service. "Ski Area Master Development Plans." https://www.fs.usda.gov/detail/whiteriver/landmanagement/planning/?cid=stelprdb5333326

U.S. Geological Survey. "Mount Bachelor." https://www.usgs.gov/volcanoes/mount-bachelor.

U.S. Ski and Snowboard Hall of Fame. "Nelson Bennett." https://skihall.com/hall-of-famers/nelson-bennett/.

Vandevert, Claude. "Vandevert Ranch History." Vandevert Ranch. March 1971. http://vandevertranch.org/history.html.

Interviews and Correspondence

Bowerman, Jay. Interviews and correspondence with author, February 2022.

Cammack, Frank. Interview with author, January 2022.

Hanson, Tor. Correspondence and discussions with author, March–June 2022.

Healy, Tom. Correspondence and discussions with author, April–June 2022.

Jaffe, Dan. Correspondence with author, January 2022.

Joslin, Les. Correspondence with author, January–August 2022.

Lomax, Tom. Correspondence with author, June 2022.

Mathews, Bob. Interviews and correspondence with author, February–May 2022.

Meissner, Jane. Interview with author, March 2022.

Oliphant, Dennis. Interview with author, January 2022.

Rathbun, Dave. Interview with author, May 2022.

Schiemer, John. Correspondence with author, April–May 2022.

Stenkamp, Steve. Discussions with author, February–July 2022.

Wesseler, Richard. Correspondence and discussions with author, March–May 2022.

Woodward, Bob. Interview with author, February 2022.

INDEX

J

Jaffe, Dan 12, 13, 137
Janney, Matt 98

K

King, Suzanne 122, 131
Kirby Nagelhout Construction
    Company 89
Klamath, the (trophy) 118, 119
Klug, Chris 123, 126
Kostol, Chris 45, 46, 47, 50

L

Lafferty, Mike 122, 125
logging 12, 16, 40, 41, 45, 55, 56,
    70, 93, 112, 120, 132
Lucas, Peggy Chessman 11, 105

M

Marcoulier, Felix 56, 66, 90
Marshall, Robert 110
Marsh, David 65, 87, 90, 91, 93,
    96
master development plans 115
Mathews, Bob 12, 13, 74, 78, 141
Mazamas 12, 13, 24, 36
McArthur, Lewis 9, 10
McCallum, Don 70
McKenzie Pass 48, 49, 119
Meissner, Jack 64, 73, 79, 123, 128
Meissner, Virginia 64, 73, 79, 80,
    135
Mohla, David 84
Monteith, Jim 84, 85
Morgan, Jop 63

Mountain Hardwear 95
Mountain hemlock 25
Mount Bachelor Observatory 12,
    137
Mount Bachelor Volcanic Chain
    21, 22, 24
Mt. Bachelor Sports Education
    Foundation 12, 77, 118, 122
Murray, Oscar 56, 57, 73, 143, 144

N

National Environmental Policy Act
    112, 116
National Forest Ski Area Permit Act
    100, 113
Native Americans 8, 35, 36
Newberry Caldera 20, 42
Newberry, John Strong 23
Nordeen, Emil 45, 46, 47, 56, 118,
    119, 123, 142
Nordic Center 12, 73, 74, 77, 99,
    101, 122, 130, 135, 144

O

Oliphant, Dennis 12, 77, 101, 122,
    142
Oregon Geographic Names Board
    9, 10
Oregon Wilderness Coalition 84
Organic Act 108
Outdoor Recreation Resources
    Review Commission 111

P

Papé, Dean 72, 87, 90, 93
Papé, Randy 96

W

Y

ABOUT THE AUTHOR

Glenn Voelz served for twenty-five years in the United States Army as an intelligence officer and spent over a decade living and working across Asia, Europe, the Middle East and Africa. During his career, he held senior leadership positions at the Pentagon on the Joint Chiefs of Staff, in the White House Situation Room and at NATO headquarters.

Glenn is a graduate of the United States Military Academy at West Point and served on the faculty as an assistant professor in the Department of History. He is the author of over a dozen books and journal articles, including three novels. When not writing, Glenn works as a professional ski patroller at the Mt. Bachelor Nordic Center and as a volunteer member of the Deschutes County Sheriff's Office Search and Rescue team.